Horse Racing

Peter Churchill

Horse Racing

BLANDFORD PRESS
Poole   Dorset

First published in the UK 1981
Copyright © 1981 Blandford Press Ltd,
Link House, West Street,
Poole, Dorset, BH15 1LL

British Library Cataloguing in Publication Data

Churchill, Peter, *b. 1933*
  Horse-racing.
  1. Horse-racing
  I. Title
  798'.4   SF334

ISBN 0 7137 1016 0 (Hardback edition)
ISBN 0 7137 1115 9 (Paperback edition)

Typeset in Monophoto Apollo $10/10\frac{1}{2}$ pt.
by Asco Trade Typesetting Ltd., Hong
Kong

Printed in Hong Kong by
South China Printing Co.

Contents

Acknowledgements

Colour Photographs

Colour Library International: plates 57, 58
Colorific: plates 23, 38, 39
Bernard Gourier: plates 8, 9, 10, 11, 14, 15, 16, 27, 36, 37, 40, 41, 42, 43, 45, 46, 47, 48, 49, 50, 51, 52, 53, 54, 55, 56
David Hastings: plates 13, 17, 18, 19, 20, 22, 24, 25, 26, 30, 34, 35, 67
Keystone Press Agency: plate 44
Mary Evans Picture Library: plates 1, 2, 3, 4, 5, 6, 7
W.W. Rouch & Co. Ltd: plate 12
Sporting Pictures: plates 21, 28, 29, 31, 32, 33, 64, 65, 66, 68, 69
Royal Hong Kong Jockey Club: plates 59, 60, 61, 62, 63

Black and White Photographs

Australian Information Service: pages 135, 138, 139, 163, 165
BBC Hulton Picture Library: pages 16, 24, 25, 26
Japan Racing Association: pages 141, 144
Keeneland Association: pages 58, 60, 115, 116, 117
Mary Evans Picture Library: page 13
Royal Hong Kong Jockey Club: page 147
W.W. Rouch & Co. Ltd: pages 27, 29, 43, 123, 152, 153, 155
Sport & General Press Agency: pages 38, 44, 56, 117, 156, 159, 160

1
The Origins of Horse Racing

The glamorous world of horse-racing – a world where fortunes are won and lost, where dreams can come true and where hopes can be shattered – has fascinated man since the earliest times. Horse-racing, the sport of kings and the downfall of princes, can mean different things to different people. To some it is a game of chance, to others a medium of social opportunity and to another group a sport of skill and speed. But is it such a game of chance and social climbing? For centuries, thought, care, science and enterprise have gone into the creation of the most vital ingredient of racing ... the thoroughbred racehorse.

The urbane ancient Greeks enjoyed the spectacle of horses racing. At the Olympic Games over 2,600 years ago horse-races on the flat with young jockeys urging their mounts to victory and glory were a popular part of the programme. The earlier Hittites, Assyrians, Urartians and Egyptians of the second millennium BC enjoyed the sport of racing horses. What form these early races took or what type of horse was used is hard to clarify, but in the Middle East it is almost certain that the prototype of the oriental horse were used. As far back as 1,400 BC settled man had brought the breeding of warm-blooded horses* under his control and was recording pedigrees.

Later, the organized Romans flocked to the local hippodrome to watch chariot races which were a dramatic form of horse-racing, living on today in trotting and pacing. Many of the drivers were professionals and teams either raced for material gain or were retained by some rich patrician to represent his stud or stable at the arena races. Jockeys' racing colours can be said to date from this era, for some of the drivers wore decorated tunics or carried special markings on their chariots so that the public and their patrons could identify them during a race. The Romans even had their version of the starting stalls with each runner standing in a wooden-framed pen for the start of each race.

---

* *Warm (or Hot)-blooded*: A term applied to horses possessing Arabian or Thoroughbred blood in their breeding lines. *Cold-blooded* indicates heavy horses such as Shires and Clydesdales.

Flat-racing was brought to ancient Britain by the conquering Roman armies and race-meetings were staged at York and Chester. At that time fast, tough ponies were bred in Scotland and known as 'Galloways' or 'Running Horses'. But apart from its entertainment value very little thought was given to the organization of the sport or the development of the horses used. This form of racing continued throughout the Middle Ages with Galloways and Hobbies, small active horses bred in Ireland, as the racehorses of the day. But the twelfth century Crusaders, and later the Tudors, began to bring oriental horses, most of them crosses between Arabain and Barb strains, into England to improve their native stock. We know very little about the organization or style the sport might have taken in those days, or indeed whether the injection of eastern blood had much influence on the Running Horses. But the spirit of racing does not seem to have changed so much over the centuries.

A twelfth century writer gives us this description of races staged outside one of London's city gates ... '... the boyes which ride the horses ... do runne races for wagers, with a desire for praise or hope of victorie.' While another gives us a fuller account ... 'Two or three boys are set on horseback to ride a race. The signal being given, they set off and push their horses to their utmost speed, sparing neither whip nor spur, urging them on at the same time with loud shouts and clamours to animate their endeavours and call forth all their powers.' But it was not until the England of James I (seventeenth century) that a truly organized pattern of racing began to emerge and the basis of the sport became tough, gruelling match-races often run in heats on the same day.

It was through the Stuart kings that two developments occurred which, over the centuries, were to lead to the creation of one of the most important sporting/leisure industries of today, and the modern multi-million dollar syndicated thoroughbred racehorse.

For it was at this time that the importation of oriental stallions and mares began: the Royal Studs set up by the Tudors and Stuarts at Hampton Court, Malmesbury, Eltham and Tutbury were the biggest and the best stocked in England. Most of them stood Arabs, Barbs or near-eastern blood stallions covering Spanish or native mares. James I, a hunting man rather than a racing man, and not all that lucky as an owner or breeder, set up a hunting lodge at Newmarket so starting the Royal connection with the East Anglian town, now the head-quarters of British flat-racing.

Later came Oliver Cromwell who not only brought the life of James' son Charles I (creator of the first Cup race at Newmarket in 1634) to a dramatic end but also 'outlawed' horse-racing, dispersing the royal stallions and mares around the country. Some went to private commercial breeders for Cromwell's objection to racing did not prevent him being interested in the improvement of horse-breeding, but many disappeared without trace.

But England soon became England again with the restoration of the monarchy in the shape of Charles II in 1660. Where James I was unlucky, this king was not only lucky but a dedicated supporter of racing. Although not a breeder himself King Charles II owned many good horses and often rode in matches and races himself. Through him, Newmarket became the true centre of the sport with his royal court staying at the town for long periods of the year. Charles II encouraged the importation of eastern stallions to form the basis for the breeding of a racehorse.

Races at this time were run as matches or plates. A match would be between two or three horses but often they ran in heats with a final, over a total distance of usually up to 2 miles, and run on the same day! A plate was a race of two, three or more horses over a laid-out, usually flagged, course where the organizer of the race, often the king himself or a member of his court, guaranteed so much prize money. In a modern plate the racecourse guarantees the prize money but keeps the entrance fees, etc. The entry fees in a modern sweepstake, plus forfeits, etc. are added to the prize money and distributed to the owners of the placed horses. Wagering on the result of a match or plate was in the seventeenth century as much an attraction of the sport as it is in most parts of the world today. Charles II created the round course at Newmarket and the racecourse became a lively centre of rivalry between the Northern-bred and trained horses and those from the South of England.

But a more important figure, more shadowy perhaps than the gregarious Charles, came onto the racing scene at this time. Tregonwell Frampton (1641–1727) was trainer manager to Charles II, a post he retained under William III, Queen Anne and King George I and II. He became, after his first patron's death, the organizing brains of horse-racing. Although there were many stories of Tregonwell Frampton being involved in 'fixed' races and 'shady' deals, his talent and ability for producing good racehorses led to William III appointing him keeper of the Royal Running Horses thus making him the first professional trainer that we know something about.

Horse-racing for some reason seems throughout its colourful history to have been closely involved with politics and religion. Perhaps this is because of the association of the ownership of horses with power and influence. For example, William III insisted that any horse owned by a Roman Catholic worth more than £5 (about $9) should be confiscated. At the same time he founded the Royal Stud at Hampton Court as an establishment specializing in the production of racehorses. In 1740 the English Parliament passed an Act restricting racing because it had grown too popular for the good of the country in the view of the then members. The Act proclaimed that no plate should be contested for £50 or over and, as we will see later, various religious-oriented movements in the New World of the United States took an anti-racing line.

All this politiking and the fact that the sport soon grew in the eighteenth century too big and popular to survive on royal patronage and adjudication alone meant that a group of men of rank and opulence formed the English Jockey Club in 1751 as the governing body of all racing in the British Isles. It was this format that became the basis of the organization of the sport in most parts of the world.

By the late eighteenth to mid-nineteenth centuries, the members of Jockey Club, the stewards of which were elected by their fellow members, began to realize that they had on their hands a sport capable of appealing to the popular imagination, and a developing breeding industry that was able to produce a pure thoroughbred racehorse.

Three men in particular were responsible for building the foundations of the structure of racing as we know it today. All three have gone down in sporting history as the 'great dictators' of the turf. Sir Charles Bunbury (1740–1821), a close friend of the Duke of York and creator of the English Derby Stakes with the twelfth Earl of Derby, after whom the great classic is named, was a successful breeder producing Doimed to win the first running of the Derby in 1780. The others were Lord George Bentinck (1802–1848) and Admiral the Hon. Henry John Rous (1795–1877).

Lord George Bentinck was a keen gambling man but a fair-minded and progressive thinker. Two events in turf history give us some clue to the man's personality. In 1836 his lordship nominated a horse called Elis to run in the St Leger, the last of the English classic races each season, staged to this day on Doncaster racecourse in the north of England. The horse was trained at Goodwood, Sussex in the south of England some 230-odd miles from Doncaster. Four days before the race Bentinck placed a bet of £1,000 at 12–1 with a bookmaker on Elis to win the Leger. The bookmaker, knowing the horse was down in the south, was confident of his Lordship's money as he thought the long walk to Doncaster would be too much for the animal. (Racehorses

Lord George Bentinck.

were 'walked' to race-meetings in those days often resting overnight on the way.) But Bentinck had a secret plan, he had arranged for a horsebox to be designed and built on wheels with a padded compartment for Elis and to be pulled by six carriage horses. The carriage horses were changed each day on the journey north and Elis arrived at Doncaster fit and well and duly won the race. So not only was this one of the greatest betting coups in the history of the sport, for today it would be worth some quarter of a million pounds, but it was also the first evidence of horse-transporters being used to get racehorses to the tracks.

But Lord George Bentinck did a great deal to rid British racing of the definitely shady reputation it was gaining in the 1840's. As one Court Judge was reported to have said during that time, '... if gentlemen condescend to race with blackguards, they must condescend to expect to be cheated ...'

His remark related to the great Derby scandal of 1844 when a horse called Running Rein, owned by a London-based gambler and trainer called Goodman Levy, and Epsom corn merchant called Anthony Wood, came home the winner of the Epsom Derby. The horse was disqualified by the stewards and prior to the race Bentinck had amassed considerable evidence to prove that Running Rein was in fact a four-year-old named Maccabeus. Wood apparently was not aware of the switch, but Levy owned both the real Running Rein and Maccabeus, changing one to the other's name in 1842.

Bentinck first started getting interested in the affair when 'Running Rein' (in fact Maccabeus) won a 2-year-old race at Newmarket beating a horse belonging to the Duke of Portland. Portland thought the winner was a well-developed 3-year-old and lodged an objection to the result but the Newmarket stewards over-ruled the objection. Bentinck, however, agreed with Portland and decided to spend his winter months investigating the background to 'Running Rein'. Five days before the 1844 Derby Lord Bentinck presented the Epsom stewards with a petition requesting them to investigate the identity of the horse called 'Running Rein'. But the stewards decided the horse should be allowed to run and if he should win they would withold the stake money pending an inquiry. 'Running Rein' ran and won, beating Orlando owned by Colonel Peel, brother of the Tory Prime Minister Sir Robert Peel. On advice from Lord Bentinck, Col. Peel called for the stewards to open an inquiry but as Goodman Levy could not be found it was adjourned indefinitely.

So Peel took court action against Wood, and Lord Bentinck produced his evidence in the case. Bentinck had suspected that

Maccabeus's legs had been dyed so he went to see every chemist and hairdresser situated between Levy's home and the club he went to everyday. He found a hairdresser by the name of Rossi who told him that he (Rossi) had sold some hair-dye to Goodman Levy. When His Lordship asked for the horse to be examined, Wood withdrew from the case. Levy and Wood were banned from the Turf, 'Running Rein' was retired and Orlando was declared the winner of the 1844 Derby.

In appreciation of his services a public subscription was started and raised £2,100 but Bentinck refused to accept any money or reward. So in 1847 it was decided that the money should be used to create a charitable fund for any licensed trainers or jockeys, or their dependents, who had fallen on hard times and it is now known as the Bentinck Benevolent Fund.

Admiral Rous, the third of the 'great dictators' of the turf, was perhaps the most influencial and forward-thinking of them all. Apart from his own racing activities, his membership of the Jockey Club, his official post as Handicapper, he also found time to publish the authoritive 'On The Laws and Practice of Horse Racing' in 1850.

The *Racing Calender*, which made its debut in 1778 and is published weekly by Weatherby & Sons, secretaries to The Jockey Club and keepers of the *Match-Book*, began to change from the 'match-race' system to shrewdly framed races over varying distances and handicaps. This in particular appealed to the growing following that was being attracted to racing, and the public quickly realized that weight allowances gave a fairer result to certain races. Handicap races also opened up a new betting market and bookmakers acquired a certain respectability from the masters of the racing game. The first handicap, known as the Oatlands Stakes, was run at Ascot racecourse in 1791, the year that the firm of Weatherbys published on behalf of the Jockey Club the first *General Stud Book*. In 1795 a man named Ogden became the first bookmaker to operate on a racecourse by setting up his pitch at Newmarket. Jockeys' racing colours were declared essential and first registered in October 1762. The Duke of Cumberland selected purple as his colours, which is still part of the British royal colours. All racing colours, jacket and cap, must be registered with Weatherbys for horses running in Great Britain and each is exclusive to the owner.

Races such as the 2,000 Guineas, Derby and St Leger were recognized as classic races for three-year-old colts and became the Triple Crown of English racing. Fillies were, and still are, allowed to run. In addition the fillies had, as now, their classic programme in the 1,000 Guineas and the Oaks. Two-year-olds, mere babies, racing along a

The Oatlands Stakes, 1791. After F.M. Sartorius, (Rischgitz).

straight sprint track became a popular format with breeders and the racing public. For many at that time, they became too popular, with even *The Times* newspaper entering the argument referring to '. . . the monstrous development of Two-year-old races . . .'. But already the trend towards speed, and more speed, was beginning to take hold.

In the mid-eighteenth century, two-year-olds were unheard of in racing but by the mid-nineteenth century more than one-fifth of the horses running were two-year-olds, while more than half of the total number of horses racing could be graded into the two and three-year-old groups. Many felt that this racing of immature animals was bad for the sport and the future of bloodstock breeding. Restrictions were imposed on two-year-old racing, but the autocratic governor of British racing, Admiral Rous, soon had these modified and the whole thing was quietly dropped a few years later. By 1873, two-year-olds were permitted to race at the beginning of season in March, much the same as they are in British racing today.

Rous – autocrat though he was – was certainly no fool or dogmatic tyrant – for in the history of Turf, not only in Britain but elsewhere too, he stands out as one of the few traditional men of rank and opulence to appreciate that the time demanded changes and that changes in turn mean progress. He was shrewd enough to realize that the sport could not resist new developments. Changes there certainly were, for in 1762, 261 races, including 49 matches were run on 76 racecourses in Great Britain with a total value of £61,440. But by 1842, 1,218 races were run, 86 of them matches, for a total prize-money of £198,990, and by 1849, 1,307 horses ran in public on 111 racecourses, 271 of them for two-year-olds, 417 for three-year-olds, 254 for four-year-olds and 265 for five-year-olds and upwards. There were some 200 Thoroughbred stallions standing at stud farms, and 1,100 brood-mares with a foal production of 830 per year.

Admiral Rous devised the first weight-for-age scale in 1850 by for example estimating that a four-year-old should give a two-year-old 37 lbs over a distance of 6 furlongs. Although he later changed this particular scale to 34 lbs. Although Rous published his calculations in 1850 and 1866, they did not become official until after his death when the scale was published in the *Racing Calendar* during 1880.

But the discerning Rous' reputation spread way beyond the shores of England. For when he was a Captain he visited Australia in 1827 to 1828. Horse-racing and Thoroughbred breeding had already started some years before but there is no doubt that the visit and influence of Rous gave the development of the sport a powerful impetus. It was his advice and knowledge of the sport that contributed, at least in part, to the then Governor Sir Ralph Darling setting up the Australian Racing and Jockey Club, taking much of the power-base away from the already organized Sydney Turf Club. This in turn led to the decisive step of forming the all-powerful Australian Race Committee in 1840. At a Sydney Agricultural Society dinner given to mark Captain Rous's visit, Sir John Jamison said that ... '... in future years when our races will emulate those of the mother country the genealogies of our best horses will be interwoven with the names of those introduced by Captain Rous.' He was to be proved right for the enthusiastic Rous imported to Australia a stallion called Emigrant, which also became known as Rous's Emigrant, and an Arab stallion named Rainbow, after the ship Captain Rous commanded at the time.

Emigrant, a good-looking brown horse with powerful hindquarters, became the most important breeding factor in the creation of some of Australia's most potent blood-lines found in the international blood-stock industry of today.

It was yet another Englishman that was largely responsible for the development of racing in France. Lord Henry Seymour was born in Paris in 1805 and spent his entire life in France. He was the son of the third Marquess of Hertford and a great friend of Ferdinand Philippe, Duc d'Orleans and heir to the French throne. Although he had an eccentric nature with a passion for practical jokes, which were not always appreciated by his socialite friends, he can be said to be the true father of French racing.

There had been some racing before the French Revolution but the French royalty were not really interested in the sport. Even when Louis XIV set up the State Stud Administration Service there was no intended policy to breed racehorses. Charles X, though, was the first French member of the royal family to show any interest in the sport. In 1776 the first uniform racecourse was laid out on the Plaines des Sablons and races were organized by the Duc de Chartres, the Comte d'Artois and the Marquis de Conflans. But then came the Revolution (1789–1795) and the Napoleonic Wars (1792–1815); racing disappeared almost without trace.

Thoroughbred stallions were being imported from England by 1817–18 but it was the earnestness of Seymour that got French racing off to its first real start. The French Jockey Club was formed in 1833 with Seymour as its first president. The idea, at the time and certainly in Seymour's eyes, was that the club should be a race committee and a social club. But Seymour and his close friend Ferdinand Philippe soon realized that the members prefered card games to racing and the breeding of bloodstock. So, only a few months after taking the presidency of the French Jockey Club, Seymour and Philippe formed the Société d'Encouragement par l'Amerlioration des Races de Chevaux en France (better known as the Société d'Encouragement) to administer and rule racing in France. The Jockey Club then became the most chic and exclusive social club in Paris but with absolutely no powers over racing. The Société d'Encouragement was recognized by the government in 1834 and the Champs-de-Mars, now the site of the Eiffel Tower on the left bank of the River Seine, became its first official racecourse staging its opening meeting on Sunday, May 4 of that year.

In the 1820s the sophisticated Parisians flocked to watch races at the dusty Champs-de-Mars and the pastoral Bois de Boulogne in the centre of the city. In 1836 a new course was created at Chantilly, just outside the city limits, which founded the Prix du Jockey Club (French Derby). As an owner Seymour won the French Derby four times, the last time was with Poetess in 1841, later one of the greatest broodmares in the history of racing.

Lord Henry Seymour and the Duc d'Orleans dominated the development of French racing and breeding until 1842 when d'Orleans died after a fall from his carriage. A disappointed Seymour sold up his entire stable.

Although the early settlers on the eastern seaboard of the USA loved their racing, it is generally accepted that yet another Englishman gave American racing its serious start in 1665. The first thoroughbreds had arrived in Virginia in 1620. Racemeetings along English lines were held on a racecourse called New Market as early as 1664. (This course was only a few miles from the now famous New York tracks of Aqueduct and Belmont Park.) In 1665 Richard Nicolls captured New Amsterdam from the Dutch, changed its name to New York and became the city's first English Governor. The following year Nicolls established the first regular racecourse in the New World at Salisbury Plain, later known as Kemstead Plain, Long Island. Governor Nicolls offered a silver cup for a race to be run over this course, but it was not until some years after the War of Independence (1775–1783) that the sport and the thoroughbred became more widespread. Many English stallions were imported to create the American Thoroughbred and two in particular had the greatest influence. They were Medley, who became a very successful sire of brood mares, and Diomed, sire of Sir Archie (foaled 1805) one of America's first great racehorses.

By the middle of the nineteenth century racing was well on the way to becoming a big international sport. In the 1860's the great English jockey, Fred Archer, travelled regularly to France to ride on the Paris tracks. In 1864 the French-bred Fille d'Air became the first French horse to win an English classic when she won the Oaks at Epsom. The following year the great Gladiateur, owned by Comte Frédéric de Lagrange one of the most important breeders in the history of French racing, became the first French horse to win the English Triple Crown (2,000 Guineas, Derby and St Leger) taking the Grand Prix de Paris in the same year. A statue of Gladiateur now stands just inside the entrance to Longchamp racecourse in Paris.

The year 1869 saw the first running of the German Derby in Hamburg. In the 1850's American owners started to invade British racing with some measure of success.

Pleased with the earlier results his American horses were getting, Pierre Lorillard sent a batch of US-bred yearlings to be trained at Newmarket in 1879. Among them was a colt called Iroquois who went on to win the 1881 Epsom Derby and became not only the first American horse to win the Blue Riband of the English Turf but one of the first to prove that the American horse was as good as his European cousins.

That same year Wall Street tycoon James R. Keene's Foxhall won the Grand Prix de Paris, the English Cesarewitch and Cambridgeshire, then trained on the following year to win the Ascot Gold Cup. By the turn of the century the American horse was really becoming a force to be reckoned with on the European racing circuit: Sibola was the winner of the 1899 1,000 Guineas, Cap and Bells II winner of the 1901 Oaks, Norman III and Sweeper II winners of the 2,000 Guineas in 1908 and 1912, and Tracery, winner of the 1912 St Leger. These horses consolidated the reputation of the American thoroughbred started by Iroquois and Foxhall.

The standing of horses from the USA was so high that several British breeders had started to import American mares (as well as French and Australian) to improve the quality and soundness of their own stock. But when anti-betting legislation virtually killed the thoroughbred industry in America in the first ten years of this century, the British and French racing authorities were alarmed at the thought of the European market being flooded with American-bred horses many of whom they considered to be of doubtful origins. Human nature being what it is, the French and British Jockey Clubs decided that action must be taken to protect their own, and their breeders', future interests. The net result was a new direction being introduced in 1913 by Weatherbys, publishers of the *General Stud Book*, which stated that, '. . . no horse or mare can, after this date, be considered as eligible for admission unless it can be traced without flaw on both sire's and dam's side of its pedigree to horses and mares themselves already accepted in the earlier volumes of the *Book*.'

This was the Jersey Act, named after the 7th Earl of Jersey, who introduced it as a resolution in 1913 to the British Jockey Club with the full agreement of his fellow members. Although it also had some affect on French breeders, which they were not too pleased about, the French racing authorities brought in a similar regulation. So the 'Jeresy Act', in effect, put up a blockade on American-bred horses in Europe as many of them could not meet the conditions of entry in the *General Stud Book*.

The American breeders were furious at the passing of the act which they saw as a blatant protectionist measure, which of course it was, designed to discriminate against some of their best home-bred horses. This was especially so in the case of all progeny descended from their great champion Lexington, for he was of doubtful origin on his dam's side (according to the new conditions of entry). But when the 'Act' was eventually repealed in 1949, it was soon apparent that it had a more negative effect on the British bloodstock industry than it had on either the American or French industries. The measure had encouraged, if not forced, other racing nations to establish their own Thoroughbred Stud Books and develop their own breeding industries independently of British stock. It was also found that some of the most successful French blood-lines were not eligible after World War II. It is ironic, in many ways, that this should have happened for between 1949 and the present time many of the world's classic and major races have been won by American-bred horses or horses of American blood-line origins, which, but for the stroke of a pen, might still be technically classified as half-breds!

In the early days, racing men of opulence and rank reigned supreme, the large influential stud farms, most of them owned by them, were stocked with race-mares carefully bred down a certain blood-line. The main object of the stud was to continue these family lines according to the breeding policy formulated by the owner. But today, to meet modern demands for a sophisticated economic efficiency, the stud farm and its managerial policy is geared more to international commercial production. Some specialize in the foal market, others in the yearling market. Many modern studs are owned by syndicates or limited companies working alongside the state owned national studs which carefully plan their breeding programmes according to the racing performance of world-wide blood-lines. A foal can now be conceived in one country, born in another, raced in a third and stand as a stallion in yet another. Such is the small but highly intensified world of bloodstock breeding today, a world that has become big business, with stallions being syndicated for millions of dollars. The expert, the racing manager, the bloodstock agent and the share consultant, with the management consultant, veterinary consultant and the therapeutist are now today's men of rank.

Many countries have recognized the stud farm's place in the scheme of things, particularly in relation to agricultural economics and the earning of foreign currency. But it is interesting, if not remarkable, that Great Britain, the birthplace of the clean-bred racehorse, does not recognize him as an agricultural product. Yet British breeders have an export record equal, in relative figures and values, to that of many industrialists and food-producers. Nevertheless, many countries, either through private enterprise or government involvement, have found a National Stud a vital means of improving thoroughbred stock.

But all this scientific breeding under modern techniques is to no avail if there is not an internationally accepted test-bed for proving their 'racing machines'. The racecourse is the stage where the performers are tested. The framing of the race-programme is not only calculated to entertain the racing public but also to encourage the expansion of the sport through investment in breeding stock.

In the early post World War II years the English Thoroughbred lost much of its predominance to the Irish-, American- and French-bred Thoroughbred on the racecourse. There were several reasons for this: the economic climate of the period cut drastically the number of big, powerful private studs, and various fiscal measures discouraged many leading breeders from investing in the future. Handicaps, that is to say races where horses are allotted weights according to their ability, never had any particular importance in the scheme of British racing, whereas the USA and Australia had already accepted that valuable handicaps were a vital part of racing and that no horse was a true champion until he had succeeded in giving weight and a beating to other good horses in a Handicap. In Britain the Handicap race was seen as a chance for the third-rate horse to come and beat, through a weight allowance, a very good horse.

In the early 1960's the Committee on the Pattern of Racing, chaired by the Duke of Norfolk, took on the job of studying the general programme of races in Great Britain with a particular emphasis on the top-class horses of all ages, and the advancement of the thoroughbred. The Committee advised:

> The Turf Authorities must ensure that a series of races, over the right distances at the right time of the year, are available to test the best horses of all ages, and they must attempt to ensure that the horses remain in training long enough and race often enough to be tested properly for constitution and soundness. The Pattern of Racing must combat the temptation to syndicate horses for stud too early in their careers ... Only by the racecourse test can the value of any individual thorougbred for breeding purpose be assessed ... and speed is the primary and indispensable criterion of excellence in the Thoroughbred ...

It was due to the findings of this committee and a later Race Planning Committee (1967) that the system of Pattern Races, similar to that used in other countries, came about. The Pattern Race system based on the grading of some one hundred classic and international races is designed to provide a comprehensive series of tests for the best horses of all ages and to accomplish a proper balance between speed and stamina. These, in effect, have created new opportunities for three-year-olds and upwards to meet in contest more frequently on the racecourses of Europe. The *Pattern Racebook*, under the jurisdiction of the Jockey Club, the Irish Turf Club and the Société d' Encourgement, publishes each season the European series of Pattern Races.

2
The Thoroughbred

Bloodstock historians seem to divide into two schools of thought on the evolution of the thoroughbred racehorse. One school says that the most formative influence in the creation of the modern racehorse was imported eastern blood through the Arab and Barb strains of warm-blooded horses. The other school stresses the Englishness of the breed. The Duke of Newcastle, for example, one of the great stud owners of the seventeenth century, was convinced that eastern blood was the best. Most of his brood mares were of oriental origin and he claimed ... 'Spanish horses are like princes and Barbs like gentlemen in their kind.'

On the other hand, at about the same period Gervase Markham, a successful son of a successful Nottinghamshire breeder, said quite the opposite ... 'For swiftness, what nation hath brought forth that horse which hath exceeded the English? When the best Barbaries that ever were in their prime, I saw them overrun by a black Hobbie at Salisbury; yet that Hobbie was more overrun by a horse called Valentine, which Valentine, neither hunting or running, was ever equalled, yet was a plainbred English horse, both by sire and dam.'

The answer must be somewhere between the two schools of thought. For racing has existed in England since the Roman Occupation, in fact it is possible it existed before that time, and there is no doubt that there were some fine examples of running horses being bred in Yorkshire, Scotland and Ireland long before the fashion began for importing eastern blood. Further, in the breeding of racehorses, or any clean-bred strain for that matter, the various in-crosses* and out-crosses† are just as important as the more apparent sire and dam line. In other words, it is over-simplifying a very complicated process to evaluate the development of the thoroughbred racehorse on the basis of his direct male line or his direct female line.

---

* *In-crosses (or Inbreeding)*: The mating of closely related blood lines. For example, mating brother with sister, sire with daughter, or son with dam.

† *Out-crosses (or Outcrossing)*: The mating of less closely related or totally unrelated blood lines.

It can most certainly be claimed nevertheless that the influence of eastern blood did produce most of the first recorded great racehorses. Three eastern stallions in particular are generally accepted as the founding fathers of the Thoroughbred. They were the Byerley Turk, the Darley Arabian and the Godolphin Arabian, and each can be found in the male line of all thoroughbreds.

In 1689 Captian Robert Byerley brought back to England an Eastern stallion that he had captured from the Turks at the Siege of Buda. Captain Byerley rode his 'Byerley Turk' at the Battle of the Boyne but later sent his versatile horse to stand at stud in the counties of Durham and Yorkshire in the north of England. The horse, apparently, did not attract many quality well-bred mares but his grandson Tartar, a good racehorse himself, sired Herod. Herod was bred by the Duke of Cumberland in 1757 and became one of the most successful stallions in Thoroughbred history getting the winners of races to the value of £200,000, a colossal sum in the eighteenth century. The 'Herod' line became one of the most influencial in

The Byerly Turk.   After a contemporary painting.

24

The Darley Arabian.   From the painting by J.N. Sartorius.

thoroughbred bloodstock breeding programmes. Many of the modern day classic winners go back in a direct male line to Herod.

A few years later, in 1704, a Yorkshire squire by the name of Richard Darley imported a stallion from Aleppo, Syria, through his brother Thomas who was an agent and consul in the city. Thomas told his brother that the colt with a white blaze and three white feet was from one of the most esteemed races among Arab horses both by sire and dam, and this race was the Manicha. It was already thought among British breeders that the very best Arab horses came from Aleppo. The colt became known as the Darley Arabian and he was by all accounts an extremely handsome horse. Although like most of the eastern stallions imported the Darley Arabian never raced himself, he was responsible for two of the greatest Thoroughbreds of all time, Flying Childers and Eclipse.

Flying Childers, a bay horse, was bred by Leonard Childers of

25

The Godolphin Arabian.   Drawn and engraved by G. Stubbs.

Doncaster, Yorkshire, in 1714 and was sired by the Darley Arabian out of a mare called Betty Leedes, (by a horse called Old Careless out of a mare called Cream Cheeks). Old Careless, Flying Childers' maternal grandsire, was by a good horse called Spanker out of a Barbary mare, and his maternal grand-dam was by the Leedes Arabian out of the dam of Spanker, a mare called Old Morocco (also known as Old Peg) and she was sired by a Moroccan Barb. So the pedigree of this great racehorse gives us a clear example of the complicated but effective in-breeding method through his closeness to Spanker and Spanker's dam and the use of Eastern sources right down the blood line.

The legendary Flying Childers was raced by the Duke of Devonshire and described by the writers of the day as the fleetest horse that ever ran at Newmarket, or, as generally believed, was ever bred in the world. One of his greatest performances was in May 1722 when he gave 14 lbs to a horse called Fox, winner of three King's Plates, the Ladies' Plate at York and several matches, and beat him by two furlongs!

The Darley Arabian's great-great-grandson Eclipse, a brilliant race-horse, was never beaten on the racecourse. Eclipse did not start his racing career until he was 5-years-old and only one horse ever gave him a real race. This was a horse called Bucephalus, and it was said that poor Bucephalus never recovered from the effort. Eclipse was without doubt the greatest racehorse of his century, retiring to stud in 1771. His influence on the breeding of future racehorses was momentous with over 100 of his descendants being winners of the Epsom Derby.

In 1730 the Godolphin Arabian arrived in England via Paris surrounded by romantic stories concerning his discovery and origins. One story claimed that he had been found pulling a cart along the cobbled streets of Paris. But, in fact, he was shrewdly purchased by Edward Coke from Derbyshire. Four Arabian horses had been given to the King of France by the Bey of Tunis, three of them were turned

Eclipse. From a contemporary print.

out in the forests of Brittany to improve the native stock there and the fourth, Godolphin, was sold to Coke. The Godolphin, a brown horse foaled in 1724, was generally accepted to be a pure-bred Jilfan Arabian and was later acquired by the 2nd Earl of Godolphin. Like his cousins, the Byerley Turk and the Darley Arabian, it seems almost certain that he never raced but was used purely for breeding. He was 29-years-old when he died on the Earl's Cambridgeshire stud farm but from him have come such good racehorses as Hurry On, Precipitation and the post-World War II Derby winner Santa Claus. The Godolphin's bloodline has exercised an effective influence on the twentieth century thoroughbred in New Zealand but perhaps his most important and potent influence was the establishing of the brillaint 'Matchem' line. Matchem was sired by Cade who in turn was sired by the Godolphin Arabian and out of a famous mare called Roxana. Matchem was an excellent honest horse and the eighteenth century breeders used to say, '. . . Snap for speed and Matchem for truth and daylight.' (Snap, a grandson of Flying Childers, was an exceptionally fast horse.) Matchem became a leading stallion and his progeny collected £151,000 in prize money.

By about 1770 the English Thoroughbred had begun to establish himself as a clean-bred strain and the importation of oriental stallions for the purposes of cross-breeding was gradually phased out in the breeding of racehorses.

The pre-twentieth century period was a time of truly great race-horses whose blood lives on today in the million-dollar racehorses of international racing. To decide which was the greatest is always difficult for each season seemed to produce a colt or filly that would not be disgraced in today's more standardized world of international Pattern Races. But if there has to be a 'greatest' then the natural holder of that crown would be the legendary St Simon.

St Simon, a beautifully made bay horse with a traditional fine eastern head, was a real racing machine. He was said to have a perfect action with the intelligence and temperament to go with it. St Simon was foaled in 1881 by the 1875 Derby winner Galopin, out of a mare called St Angela. His dam had a very poor breeding record. It seems that it was this factor that led to his breeder, Prince Batthyany, entering him in only one of the classics, the 2,000 Guineas. But he, in fact, did not run in the race as the rules at that time barred a colt or filly from running if it had changed ownership after being entered. Prince Batthyany had died from heart failure on the steps of the Jockey Club luncheon-rooms, so the mightly St Simon was put up for sale.

The legendary St Simon.

The Duke of Portland purshased the colt at the bargain price of 1,800 Guineas, and, although the horse could not run in the classics, it turned out to be one of the most far-seeing buys His Grace could have made. St Simon won the Ascot Gold Cup and the Goodwood Cup in 1884 and finished his racing career with an unbeaten record. He was reported as having electrifying acceleration, and the finest race he ever ran was in the Ascot Gold Cup when he beat a horse called Tristan, winner of the Gold Cup the previous year and runner-up in the 1881 Grand Prix de Paris behind the great American horse Foxhall, by 25 lengths!

Fred Archer, one of racing's all-time greats and rider of Ormonde in the 1886 Derby and St Leger, always said that St Simon was the greater of the two. Mat Dawson, St Simon's trainer who sent out six Derby winners between 1860 and 1895, said that the horse was most definitely the finest he had ever handled.

At stud St Simon proved himself as good as he was on the track, by passing on to his offspring his own special qualities. He headed the list of leading stallions no less than nine times, more often than any other stallion since the 1787 Derby winner Sir Peter Teazle, who finished at the top of the list on ten occasions. St Simon sired 17 classic winners and died at the ripe old age of 27.

But there were many others that would qualify for the twentieth century title of equine superstars, great horses that created great bloodstock dynasties. These are horses such as Ormonde, winner of numerous races between 1885–7 including the British Triple Crown in 1886. Ormonde retired from the racecourse unbeaten. The mare Pocahontas, foaled in 1837 by Glencoe out of Marpessa, was the dam of Stockwell, who was styled the 'Emperor of Stallions' in his own time, King Tom and Rataplan. Persimmon, a son of St Simon, and winner of the 1896 Epsom Derby, and The Flying Dutchman, the horse that played such an important role in the creation of the French thoroughbred, were other stars of this period. The Flying Dutchman, the 1849 Epsom Derby and St Leger winner, beat Lord Zetland's Voltigeur (1850 Epsom Derby and St Leger winner) in a famous match for 1,000 Guineas at York in 1851 and many others like Mameluke, 1827 Derby winner, bred at the 5th Earl of Jersey's famous Middleton Stoney stud in Oxfordshire, Archibald, Bravura, Jerry, Vanish, The Colonel, Grey Momus, Birmingham, Velocipede, Medley and Diomed were to leave their 'Prophets thumbmark' on the twentieth century thoroughbred racehorse throughout the world.

The first Eastern stallion to arrive in the USA from England was Bulle Rocke, a son of the effective Darley Arabian, in 1730. At first, the American racehorse, like his English cousin, was a cross between imported stallions or brood mares and local stock. The injection of English blood, through Medley, Messenger and Diomed, created the mighty thoroughbred dynasties which were to dominate the New World and which all originated, through the male line, from such classic British blood as Eclipse, Matchem and Herod.

The first horse to set the standard of the American racehorse was Sir Archie, a bay horse standing 16 hh and sired by Diomed. Sir Archie was foaled in 1805 and went on to win the Jockey Club Purse at Fairfield, the Jockey Club Purse at Petersburg and followed this by running away from a high-class field at Halifax in North Carolina.

In the early nineteenth century Diomed's grandson Sir Henry was matched against American Eclipse (named after the great British racehorse and closely related to Diomed). Some 60,000 people flocked to the Union Racecourse, New York, to see the match which carried the fantastic stake of $20,000. The match was run over four heats and American Eclipse was the winner but the two horses would have raced over 12 miles against each other that day in 1823! But although Sir Archie and others were great racehorses in the USA they were still very much an imported breed.

It was not until the beginning of this century that the American Thoroughbred really started to make his mark in the world. But it was very nearly a near-miss as the European breeders (who were suffering considerable financial set-backs due to the successes of American-bred racehorses) put up a blockade against them in the form of the 'Jersey Act' (1913). The star player in this particular political game was a horse called Lexington, one of North America's most successful racehorses in the mid-1800's and went on to become one of the country's greatest sires. Lexington, who went completely blind in the last year's of his life, was champion sire 16 times and got 600 foals, nearly half of them winning a grand total of $1,159,321 in prize money. By the end of the nineteenth century practically every good racehorse in the USA had the blood of Lexington, a bay horse standing 15.3 hh, in his pedigree.

But Lexington was a great racehorse that nearly wasn't due to the protectionist European breeders, and the conditions of entry into the *General Stud Book* at that time. It was not successfully established that he was clean-bred, and it was claimed that his pedigree was doubtful on his dam's side. In effect this ruling made the great Lexington a humble half-bred by European standards. This strange situation continued until 1949 when the British Jockey Club and the *General Stud Book* repealed the 'Act' stating: 'Any animal claiming admission from now on must be able to prove satisfactorily some eight to nine crosses of pure blood, to trace back at least a century, and to show such performances of its immediate family on the Turf as to warrant the belief in the purity of its blood.'

So almost overnight the majority of American racehorses became thoroughbreds again, along with their descendents, many of whom were racing in Europe at the time. With the passing of time, evolution and scientific breeding programmes transformed the lanky, long-backed equine racing machine of the seventeenth, eighteenth and nineteenth centuries into the short-backed, well-rounded and deep racehorse of the twentieth century. One such horse, in particular brought the American thoroughbred galloping into the twentieth century. The illustrious Man O'War, for many the greatest racehorse to ever put a plated-foot on the American Turf, can be found in the lineage of such brilliant top-class European winners as Never Say Die (winner of the 1954 British classics, the Derby and St Leger), Relko (winner of the 1963 Epsom Derby) and Sir Ivor (winner of the 1968 2,000 Guineas and Derby) besides home-based champions like Buckpasser (winner of $1,462,000 in prize money) and Arts and Letters (winner of America's Belmont Stakes in 1969).

Man O'War, a fine looking chesnut with a strong character and nicknamed 'Big Red' by American racegoers, was by Mahubah out of Fair Play and was foaled in 1917. The colt was sold by his breeder August Belmont II to Pennsylvannia textile manufacturer Samuel D. Riddle for $5,000. In a 30-year career, during which he was never known to have a day's illness or leave an oat of feed, 'Big Red' earned more than one million dollars from prize money, stud fees and sales of his foals. Among his off-spring were the Belmont Stakes winners American Flag and Crusader, and the gallant little Battleship that won the English Grand National Steeplechase in 1938. The tough chesnut was only beaten once in 21 starts which included winning the Belmont Stakes and Preakness Stakes in 1920, and breaking seven American and World track records as a three-year-old.

The Australian Thoroughbred had a slightly less chequered development but nonetheless there is a parallel with the American racehorse in so much as the Australian (or more correctly the Australasian) Thoroughbred has worked his way to the top-end of the international bloodstock market in the last 20 years.

The first record of horses arriving on the continent was a shipment brought by early English settlers with the First Fleet in January, 1788. But it was some years before the arrival of the first stock was to provide the foundation of the Australasian bloodhorse. The English Thoroughbred stallion Rockingham was sent from South Africa in 1799 and put to stud in New South Wales. Many of the broodmares used were imported from South Africa and these, along with local mares, were the tap-root stock for the Australian racehorse. The first English Thoroughbred stallion to be imported direct from England was Northumberland in 1802. Northumberland, and an Arab stallion called Hector imported from Calcutta, were the leading sires in Australia up to 1820. But a number of eastern stallions were also imported from India.

But the most important shot in the arm for Australian breeding came from the then Captain Rous when he visited Australia in 1827–28. Rous imported a stallion called Emigrant, also known as Rous's Emigrant, and this horse was to become the most influential factor in creating some of the very successful Australian blood-lines.

The *Australian Stud Book* was first published in 1878 by William Yuille, a Melbourne bloodstock agent and journalist, and has been published regularly since then. Conditions of entry are on the same lines as for the *General Stud Book* but, of course, the *Australian Stud Book* had to accept a certain number of families whose origins were lost in the early colonial days. These were given entry on performance/results on the racecourse and each family accepted was given a code number for identification, for example, Australian Number 10 and so on. Many of the great Australian racehorses of this century trace to these unknown but numbered blood-lines. In the nineteenth century the rate of importation of English stallions and broodmares was stepped up and nowadays they are joined by New Zealand, Irish and American Thoroughbreds. But, throughout, Australasian breeders have gone for toughness and honesty with as much speed as possible.

New Zealand has followed very closely the policy of Australia and has formed an industry that is geared to the production of racehorses suited to the conditions of racing in Australia. The great advantage New Zealand has over her big neighbour is her perfect climate and soil conditions for the rearing of high-class horses. With the sea always in close proximity the air is good, there are no extremes of temperature; the soil is high in mineral content for the building of bone, and the rainfall is just about right for the steady growth of pasture. Under these conditions breeders can run foals out with their mares night and day, with just a pasture shelter. There is no need to stable them at night as there is no danger from the elements. The foals can then be reared naturally with their mothers until weaning and the mares lactate well, right up to weaning time. Therefore the youngsters are given a great start in life with all the healthy growth ingredients that only a natural system can give them.

Three of the most famous, and perhaps greatest, racehorses in the history of the Australian Turf were New Zealand-bred. These were Carbine, Phar Lap and Tulloch and between them they cover a period of racing history from 1885 to the 1950's. Carbine was foaled in New Zealand and apart from a highly successful racing career, including winning the Melbourne Cup, he sired the winners of over 200 races.

Phar Lap was bred in New Zealand in 1926. He was by Night Raid, a fairly moderate performer in England and Australia although he had some success as a stallion. As a yearling and two-year-old Phar Lap was big and backward and for this reason he was gelded. But at that time geldings were allowed to race in the classics and when Phar Lap went into his three-year-old season he began to show signs of maturity and the ability that was to raise him way above the average. He won the Australian Jockey Club Derby and St Leger, and the Victoria Derby and St Leger but his greatest win was carrying a huge 9 st 12 lb when taking the most prestigious race in Australia, the Melbourne Cup, as a four-year-old.

Phar Lap, the name meant 'lightning', was Australia's answer to America's Man O'War. America's legendary racing machine was known by racegoers and handlers as 'Big Red' and Australia's racetrack superstar was known as the 'Red Terror'. Phar Lap raced with success in America and Mexico where he won the Agua Caliente Handicap in the track record time of 2 mins $2\frac{4}{5}$ secs carrying 9 st 3 lb. Phar Lap's death was a sad one and a slightly mysterious one. He died while turned out and the theory was that he had eaten grass that had been sprayed with poison.

Tulloch was quite the opposite to the Red Terror. He stood only 15.2 hh and was dogged with a mysterious internal complaint all his life. Tulloch was bred at Mr D. H. Blackie's Trelawney Stud on the North Island in 1954. As a yearling he was a midget but leading Australian trainer Tommy Smith liked what he saw and bought him for a mere 750 guineas! Tommy Smith, based in Sydney and one of the few Australian trainers to win his patrons more than a million Australian dollars in one season, was soon repaid for his shrewdness. Tulloch won a record £A18,088 as a two-year-old, then went on to three Derbys, the Caulfield Cup and the Brisbane Cup. In his racing career he ran 53 times winning 36 races and total stake money of £A100,000.

In more recent years the Australian/New Zealand Thoroughbred has spread his wings and established himself on the international racing scene. Two racehorses in particular have played leading roles in the expansion, Tobin Bronze who finished third in the 1967 running of the Washington International at Laurel Park, USA, and Sailor's Guide who won the International Invitation Race in 1958 after the disqualfication of Tudor Era. Sailor's Guide, although his dam was English, was a perfect example of the tough and consitent Australian produced racehorse. From 62 starts he won 19 races including the Victoria Derby and the Sydney Cup.

Meanwhile, back in Europe, the Anglo/Irish Thoroughbred was developing along a path strewn with highs, lows and back through moderate to high again. The pre-World War II years was a period of near-perfection for the English Thoroughbred with such outstanding performers as Spion Kop, Captain Cuttle, Papyrus, Felstead, Trigo, Blenheim, Hyperion, Windsor Lad, Bahram, Mahmoud and Blue Peter.

These horses were all Epsom Derby winners, taking the prestige of British bloodstock to one of its highest peaks.

But three of these great racehorses Blenheim, Bahram and Mahmoud were exported to America and one of them, Hyperion, was to contribute his line to the mighty American Thoroughbred through his two sons Heliopolis and Alibhai.

It is, perhaps, almost ironic, that it was a great European breeder who was to be instrumental in strengthening the American bloodlines after World War II. In the 1940's and 50's the Aga Khan was Europe's leading owner on no less than 13 occasions and at one time held the record of earning £1 million in stake money – a unique distinction in his day. The Ishmaelite leader was also the owner of one of the most powerful breeding operations of its time, mainly based in Ireland. He owned the winners of over 50 European classic races and bred Bahram, the 1935 Triple Crown winner, and Mahmoud, the 1936 Epsom Derby track record-holder (2 mins $33\frac{4}{5}$ secs). The Aga Khan's breeding policy of 'speed and more speed' could almost have been designed to suit the American style of racing and when, in the War years, he sold Blenheim, Mahmoud, Bahram, Hyperion's sons Alibhai and Khaled, and the super-fast but hypersensitive Nasrullah, the European bloodstock industry suffered one of its severest set-backs from which it is yet to recover. Blenheim, Mahmoud, Bahram and the others played a vital role in improving the American thoroughbred but the impact of Nasrullah was absolutely epoch-making.

Nasrullah possessed fantastic speed and, unlike many other speed-types, passed this brilliance on to his off-spring. Nasrullah had been the leading sire in England for one season but in the USA he headed the Leading Sires List five times and when he sired the colt Bold Ruler he created the prototype of the modern American racehorse. Bold Ruler was foaled in 1954 out of a mare called Miss Disco, bred down traditional American bloodlines, and as a three-year-old won the American classic, the Preakness Stakes. That year, 1957, the colt was voted Horse of the Year, and after winning 23 races from 33 starts, went on to prove himself a great stallion. The preocupation of the American classic programme with speed certainly had results in Bold Ruler, for he became one of the world's greatest sires of speedy horses and was top of the list of winning sires from 1963 to 1970.

The impact of Nasrullah's blood did not stop at Bold Ruler, for his son sired Secretariat, one of the most successful American racehorses of the last decade. Secretariat was foaled in 1970, out of a mare called Something Royal, on the Meadow Stud, Virginia owned by Mrs Penny Tweedy, daughter of the late Christopher Chenery of Meadow Farm.

The good-looking chesnut, Secretariat, with three white stockings and a star on his forehead, was to become in the space of two seasons the most valuable horse in the history of the USA. Trained at Belmont Park, New York, by French-Canadian Lucien Laurin and ridden in all but his final race by Ron Turcotte, this equine superstar followed up a promising two-year-old career by taking the 1973 Triple Crown, the first to do so since Citation in 1948. Secretariat, won the Kentucky Derby in a record time of 1 m 59.6 secs, went on to land the Preakness in great style and completed the third leg of the Triple Crown by an astonishing 31-length victory in the Belmont Stakes, smashing the track record at the same time.

Over 41,000 race-fans turned up to see him win the Arlington Park International, beating My Gallant by nine lengths. He rounded off his great career on the track by winning the Canadian International Champion Stakes. The chesnut then went to stud at the Claiborne Farm, Kentucky, syndicated to 32 breeders for a record $6,080,000. Secretariat goes into the record books as the richest three-year-old ever, having won the most prize-money in one season, $800,000, and his total career winnings for two seasons of $1,316,808 made him the fourth all-time money earner.

In the 1960's the mighty American dollar was all-powerful and the international net of racing was hauling into the prosperous US-bloodstock industry the choicest fillies, brood-mares and stallions from wherever they could be found in the world. The undefeated Italian Champion Ribot, the French classic horse Sea Bird II, and the British-bred Vaguely Noble, were among the vintage European products that went to the States in the swinging sixties.

Ribot, by the great Italian horse Tenerani out of Romanella and foaled in 1952, was unbeaten in 16 races. He won the Prix de l'Arc de Triomphe twice, the King George VI and Queen Elizabeth Stakes at Ascot, the Premio del Jockey Club and the Gran Premio di Milano. Bold Ruler was the finest sire of fast and early maturing stock but Ribot was certainly the 'king' of the world's stallions for producing classic horses. The brilliant Italian horse produced Ragusa, winner of the Irish Sweeps Derby, Prince Royal, winner of the Prix de l'Arc de Triomphe, Tom Rolfe, winner of the 1965 Preakness Stakes, Arts and Letters, winner of the 1969 Belmont Stakes, and Ribero and Ribocco winners of the St Leger and Irish Sweeps Derby. He was sent to the USA in 1965 on a five-year lease but when the term was finished it was decided that he was too valuable to risk the journey back to Italy so the great stallion stayed on the Darby Dan Farm, Lexington, Kentucky.

Sea Bird, bred in France, winner of the Epsom Derby Stakes and the Prix de l'Arc Triomphe in 1965, also went to the USA on the basis of a 5-year lease, so two of the greatest European-bred racehorses stood at American stud farms. Not as successful as Ribot with his progeny, Sea Bird did produce one of the greatest race-mares of modern times in Allez France-bred in the USA out of Priceless Gem. Paris-based owner Daniel Wildenstein bought her as a foal and then put her in training at his private yard in Chantilly. The flying filly won twice as a two-year-old and then went on to take the two French 'fillies' classics, the Poule d'Essai des Pouliches and the Prix de Diane. The Sea Bird filly ran in second to the English-trained Rheingold in the Prix de l'Arc de Triomphe but in 1974 in the gifted hands of French Champion jockey Yves St Martin, Allez France came out of a very tight finish to win the coveted 'Arc'.

Allez France finished her racing days at Santa Anita, California, having earned on European tracks the total prize-money of £527,258. She is now at stud in America.

Vaguely Noble, by Vienna out of Noble Lassie, was foaled in 1965 and bred by the late Major Lionel Holiday. The colt showed good juvenile promise winning the Sandwich Stakes at Ascot and the Observer Gold Cup at Doncaster but he was not entered in any of the 1968 British classics. When Major Holiday died his son Brook Holiday put Vaguely Noble, as a two-year-old, up for sale at the Tattersalls December Sales. The colt fetched 136,000 guineas, a record then for a horse in training. The successful bidder was an American bloodstock agent — Al Yank — buying on behalf of Californian surgeon Dr Robert Franklyn who later sold a half-share to the underbidder at the sale, a Texan Oil Millionaire, Nelson Bunker Hunt.

With the aim of winning the Prix de l'Arc de Triomphe, Vaguely Noble was sent to Etienne Pollet's yard at Chantilly, France. After a preliminary winning outing at Longchamp the colt went on to win the 1968 'Arc' beating the English Derby winner Sir Ivor by three lengths.

That was his final appearence in public and he was syndicated for the then world record price of $5,000,000 to stand at the Gainesway Farm, Lexington, Kentucky. Among his progeny is another great race-mare of our times, Dahlia, a winner of £552,045 in Europe and $1,543,139 in the United States. Dahlia is now at stud in Kentucky.

The American bloodstock industry was not getting it all its own way during the 1960's for E. P. Taylor, the industrial tycoon, bred Northern Dancer on his Ontario stud and brought the Canadian thoroughbred high on the World League ratings. Northern Dancer

P. Cook on Ope Totowah (right) wins the Epsom Northern Dancer Stakes.

was a very good racehorse, winning the 1964 Kentucky Derby, the Preakness, and Canada's most prestigious race – the Queen's Plate at the Woodbine Racetrack, but it was his illustrious son Nijinsky that really set the racing world alight. Charles Engelhard bought Nijinsky for $84,000 and sent him to be trained by Vincent O'Brien at Ballydoyle, County Tipperary, Ireland.

Nijinsky was one of the top racehorses of this century and became in 1970 the first British Triple Crown winner since Bahram in 1935. As a two-year-old the colt won four races in Ireland before going to Britain to run in the Dewhurst Stakes at Newmarket when he was ridden by Britain's greatest jockey – Lester Piggott – who was to be associated with most of the colt's later brilliant triumphs.

The following year he won the Gladness Stakes and the 2,000 Guineas before going on to win the Epsom Derby, Irish Derby and the St Leger, but perhaps one of his greatest performances was winning the King George VI and Queen Elizabeth Stakes at Ascot easily beating the previous Epsom Derby winner by two lengths.

The late Mr Charles Engelhard sold his magnificent Canadian colt to an American syndicate for $5,440,000 and Nijinsky was sent to stand at stud at Bull Hancock's Claiborne Farm, Kentucky.

At the moment the North American racehorse reigns supreme. Since 1968 the North American breeding industry, that is the United States and Canada, have produced 26 winners of classic races in Britain and France and six winners of the Prix de l'Arc de Triomphe. But the Anglo-Irish thoroughbred, whose forefathers started it all long ago, is not on his last legs yet. The brilliant Irish-bred British-trained Troy, winner of the 1979 British and Irish Derbys and third in the 'Arc' was rated second in that year's International Classification. This was the third International Classification compiled by the official handicappers of Britain, Ireland and France. British breeders were in fourth place as producers of top-class performers on the major racecourses of Europe. But in the three-year-old section over 10 furlongs plus, French breeders supplied three of the top rated horses: Three Troikas, winner of the 'Arc', rated first, Le Marmot, second in the 'Arc' and the French Derby, rated third, and Top Ville, winner of the French Derby, was rated fourth. Of the 120 horses included in the Classifications, Ireland accounted for 37 (30.8%), France, 34 (28.3%) and the United States of America, 27 (22.5%).

3
Racing in Great Britain and Ireland

The British did not think up the idea of racing horses for sport or gain but it was certainly in Britain that the Thoroughbred horse was created and eventually taken to the four corners of the earth. It is ironic, or perhaps, poetic justice, that this gift to the sporting world should now be bred to a higher standard and with more scientific and commercial management in countries many miles from the White Cliffs of Dover.

When the great French horse Gladiateur ran away with the British Triple Crown, the 2,000 Guineas, Derby and St Leger, in 1865, the slow but sure demolition of the tradition of the indomitable English-bred racehorse began. In the latter half of the nineteenth century British breeders were already beginning to look to other countries such as France, Australia and America for brood-mares and stallions to improve the quality and soundness of their own stock. But when the anti-betting legislation virtually brought racing and racehorse breeding in the USA to a halt in the first ten years of this century, the British Stud Book authorities and the Jockey Club thought that there was a danger of the European Market being flooded with American horses of doubtful origin. So the 'Jersey Act' came into force and Weatherbys, keepers of the *General Stud Book*, issued a new regulation, stating, '. . . no horse or mare can, after this date, be considered as eligible for admission unless it can be traced without flaw on both sire's and dam's side of its pedigree to horses and mares themselves already accepted in the earlier volumes of the Book.'

The American breeders, quite obviously, were not exactly delighted at the adoption of the 'act' and saw it as a blatant protectionist measure designed to discriminate against some of their best home-bred produce. But when the 'act' was repealed in 1949, it was soon realized that the British bloodstock industry had suffered most from this ill-conceived ruling as foreign horses, mainly French, dominated the top-end of the sport carrying off most of the English classic and championship races. Between 1946 and 1969 French-bred horses won

24, that is 20%, of the classic races staged on English racecourses.

If the Jersey Act did considerable damage to British racing by encouraging other racing nations to set up their own stud books and, by virtually leaving the door wide open for the French breeders to take their pick of the 'doubtful' bloodlines of America, giving other breeders the flexibility of choice and decision independently of British stock, there are few people in British racing today with any illusions about the urgent need to stop the outflow of prime breeding stock which looks likely to continue, thereby hastening the decline of the whole racing industry in the UK.

On the face of it, all looks well in English racing; more horses are being put in training, record prices are being paid at Yearling and Horses-in-training Sales and prize money is increasing each season. But these are only surface facts: in any industry, whether it be in the leisure market or the manufacturing market, without long-term investment geared to improving standards or quality, the future well-being and prosperity of all involved is at risk.

The poor level of prize money and the lack of breeders' incentive schemes in Britain discourage the now very efficient international racing concerns and syndicates from investing in home-raised bloodstock and horses in training. Whereas French racing, which operates under a State betting monopoly financial structure, with its high level of prize-money, even for moderate races, and its breeders' incentive schemes, not only attracts runners from all over Europe and as far away as the USA and Australia but also the new men of opulence and rank, such as the Texan Nelson Bunker Hunt, the international art dealer Daniel Wildenstein and the British millionaire Robert Sangster.

Money may indeed be the root of all evil but it is also the root of most problems in life and business. In Britain, for example, the national exchequer gets well over £100 million per annum from the duty on horse-race betting alone whereas less than £10 million of the gross amount gambled per year is put back into the sport through the Betting Levy Board, the organization responsible for allocating funds to the various sectors of the sport.

In France, on the other hand, the share going back into racing from the £370-odd million gambled each year is well over £70 million per annum. The Horserace Totalisator Board in Britain believes that the lush pickings enjoyed by the European and USA racing authorities could apply in England if the Tote could takeover all off-course betting shops leaving the private bookmakers to operate on-course only. But until some economics expert can come up with the answer as to how the Tote is going to be able to pay for the 12,000-odd betting shops, the belief is but a dream.

That the decline of British racing is a reality was heavily under-lined by the fact that in 1976 four out of five British Classic races were won by horses from abroad, as was Ascot's great championship race the King George VI and Queen Elizabeth Stakes. In 1977 the trend continued, with the exception of The Oaks.

But the times they are a-changing, albeit at a slow rate. The creation of the British Racing Industry Council (BRIC) in the autumn of 1974, largely due to the efforts of Newmarket trainer John Winter, reflected a new spirit among those dependent on the sport for their living and has given new impetus and exposure to the problems that are facing the sport in the 1980's.

Among the gloom and doom there are some bright and sparkling rays to encourage hope and optimism; English jockeys are still rated highly throughout the world; the English classics and the champion-ship races of Royal Ascot, Newmarket, Doncaster, Epsom and Sandown still hold their international prestige; and against all the odds Anglo/Irish-bred horses have maintained an impressive record of wins in major Pattern races (Group I Championship races). The Irish Pattern Races are run on their home courses for which the prize money now tops the £2 million mark. (The allocation for French Pattern races is more than double that figure, not including owners contributions, bonuses or breeders' premiums). These factors do indicate there is still time for something to be done. But it must be done quickly for the Pattern Race system, some 100 races graded in a series to test the best horses of all ages, will bring further competition for major English races from abroad in the future.

Although the North American horse has dominated the British Classic-race programme for the last few years through such great performers as Sir Ivor (The 2,000 Guineas and Epsom Derby in 1968), Nijinsky (The 1970 Triple Crown), Mill Reef (The 1971 Epsom Derby, Eclipse Stakes, King George VI and Queen Elizabeth Stakes and the Prix de l'Arc de Triomphe), Dahlia (The 1973 King George VI and Queen Elizabeth Stakes) Pawnese (The 1976 Oaks and King George VI and Queen Elizabeth Stakes) and The Minstrel (The 1977 English and Irish Derbys) these star-spangled superstars on four legs have not had it all their own way. The Anglo/Irish thoroughbred in the fine shape of Brigadier Gerard, Vaguely Noble, Grundy and Troy has had his fair share of glory too.

The well-built bay, Vaguely Noble, sire of Dahlia and 1976 Epsom Derby winner Empery, was bred in Ireland as was Leymoss. Both won Europe's most respected and valuable middle distance inter-

Vaguely Noble, Prix de l'Arc de Triomphe winner and sire of Dahlia and Empery.

national race, The Prix de l'Arc de Triomphe in 1968 and 1969.

Grundy (foaled 1972) by Great Nephew and out of Word from Lundy, was bred at the Overbury Stud, Gloucestershire. The colt was purchased by a bloodstock agent for 11,000 guineas at the 1973 Tattersalls Newmarket Yearling Sales on behalf of Dr Carlo Vittadini the Milan industrialist. Dr Vittadini sent him to be trained by Peter Walwyn at Lambourn, Berkshire, and Grundy started his racing career winning all four of his races as a two-year-old. In 1975 a training set-back upset his preparation for the first of the classics, the 2,000 Guineas at Newmarket in which he finished second. But the stable confidence grew as the colt almost walked away with the Irish 2,000 Guineas at The Curragh. But Derbys are really what the classics are all about and Grundy went to Epsom to win the English Derby under stable jockey Pat Eddery and then to the Curragh to win the Irish Sweeps Derby. All very impressive stuff but a real champion can beat the best of any age, and Grundy proved himself just such a champion when after a long, tough battle against the 1974 St Leger winner Bustino, he got to the line half-a-length up to win the King George VI and Queen Elizabeth Stakes. Grundy won a British-trained record in prize money of £326,422 and now stands at the British National Stud at Newmarket.

Brigadier Gerard, is a typical example of the spirit of 'private enterprise' in British racing shining through to beat the big, powerful and faceless international groups at their own game. Sired by Queen's Hussar out of La Paiva, the 'Brigadier' (foaled 1968) was bred by his owners John Hislop, the former champion amateur flat-race jockey and his wife Jean on their East Woodhay House Stud. The colt was trained by Berkshire-based Dick Hern and ridden throughout his career by 1979 Champion jockey Joe Mercer.

This talented colt won 17 of his 18 races and was the only British classic winner of the present century to have been unbeaten in 10 or more starts in his first two seasons. The 'Brigadier' won a grand total

Brigadier Gerard with J. Mercer up wins the 2,000 Guineas at Newmarket.

of £253,024 in prize money before retiring to stud.

Unbeaten as a two-year-old, Brigadier Gerard, beat Mill Reef, that year's Epsom Derby winner, in the 1971 2,000 Guineas at Newmarket, the only time these two great contempories raced against each other. He then went on to win four top-class mile races, including the Sussex Stakes at Goodwood, before closing his three-year-old campaign with a narrow win over the Irish colt Rarity in the Champion Stakes over $1\frac{1}{4}$ miles in very heavy going.

In 1972 the 'Brigadier' won the Lockinge Stakes, the Prince of Wales Stakes and the Eclipse Stakes which is a highly-rated international 'championship'. It was then decided to try him over the classic distance of $1\frac{1}{2}$ miles, a trip many thought beyond him. But the gamble paid off and John and Jean Hislop's colt won the King George VI and Queen Elizabeth Stakes at Ascot, one of the most important Group I Pattern Races in Europe. The 'Brigadier' ended his racing career in the style of a truly great racehorse winning the Queen Elizabeth II Stakes and for a second time the Champion Stakes at Newmarket.

The year of Troy was 1979 when he proved a shrewd investment for his owners, Sir Michael Sobell and his son-in-law Sir Arnold Weinstock. Troy also revealed the talent of the thoroughly modern jockey Willie Carson and trainer Dick Hern. This was the year when British blood pulled back some of the past glories of the mother country of the Thoroughbred. In addition was the romantic bonus that 1979 was the 200th anniversery of the running of the Epsom Derby.

Troy, a powerful colt with quality, was bred at the Ballymacoll Stud, Co. Meath, Ireland and sired by Petingo out of La Milo. The strength of his Anglo/Irish blood came from both sides of his pedigree. On his sire's side he traced back to Petition, Alycidon and Fairway, and on his dam's side he traced back to Pinza, Hyperion – 'the daddy of them all', and the great sire Gainsborough who was a male descendent of the Darley Arabian. Troy, in the hands of Willie Carson, literally ran away with the Epsom Derby beating the Irish colt Dickens Hill by seven lengths with the Canadian-bred Northern Baby, trained in France, a further three lengths away in third place. Troy went on to win the Irish Sweeps Derby, just as easily, and in spite of blotting his otherwise copy book record by being beaten in the Prix de l'Arc de Triomphe, finished up 1979 as leading racehorse with £310,539 in his connection's kitty from five races. So although the Anglo/Irish bloodstock flag may not have been flying from the very top of the pole at the end of the 1970's, it was certainly fluttering, despite the negative economic climate, with some pride and optimism as the oldest system of horse-racing faced the 1980's.

Racecourses
There are 61 racecourses in Britain, all different, all with their own individual qualities ... some on revered ground, some with industrial backcloths, some now part of modern urban leisure centres ... but all bustling with action and that special old-fashioned atmosphere unique to British racing. All the British courses have grass surfaces but each has its own particular physical characteristics, the tightness of the bends, some are left-handed, some right-handed, some are almost completely flat and others having varying undulations. The idiosyncrasies of the British weather mean a wide difference in the state of the going from one end of the country to the other varying, even in high summer, from rock-hard ground to almost a quagmire. So in Britain the old saying, 'horses for courses' is more profound than anywhere else in Europe. Most of the racecourses in Britain are steeped in history as are the five classic races, The Oaks and 1,000 Guineas for three-year-old fillies, and the 2,000 Guineas, Derby and St Leger, which make up the Triple Crown.

Ascot
The first meeting to be staged on the Berkshire Heath was in 1711 by the command of Queen Anne. The regal connection with the course has remained with the Royal Meeting, staged over four days in June each year, which is one of the main highlights of the flat-racing year. The richest race in England, the King George VI and Queen Elizabeth Stakes, is run at Ascot in July over 1 mile 4 furlongs and is now recognized as one of Europe's most important championship tests between three-year-olds and their elders during the summer. At the Royal Meeting the race-programme is an entertaining mixture of tricky handicaps and sub-classic cup races such as the Ascot Gold Cup, the Queen Alexandria Stakes, the Royal Hunt Cup, the Wokingham Stakes and the five furlong King's Stand Stakes, which attaracts some of Europe's best sprinters each year.

The stayers' 'classic' is the Ascot Gold Cup run over 2 m 4 f, it was founded in 1807 and first won by a horse called Master Jackey. From 1845 to 1853 it was known as the Emperor's Plate. Two of the longest races in British racing are run at Ascot, the Queen Alexandra Stakes and the Brown Jack Stakes, both run over 2 m 6 f 34 yd. The Ascot round course is a right-handed triangular circuit of 1 m 6 f 34 yd with a home-straight of 3 f but all races of a mile and under are run over

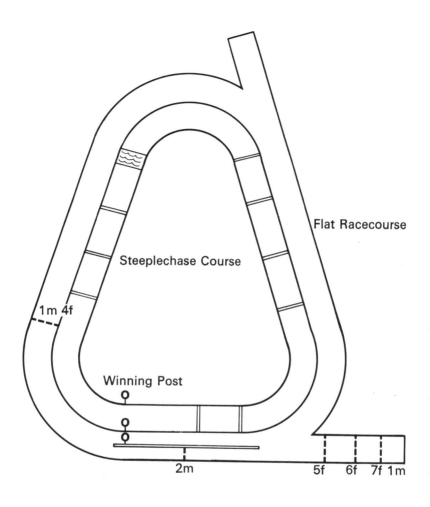

Flat Racecourse

Steeplechase Course

1m 4f

Winning Post

2m

5f   6f   7f 1m

Ascot Racecourse.

47

the straight course which is used for the Royal Hunt Cup.

Epsom
This is the home of the Derby and Oaks and perhaps one of the best known racecourses in the world. The most celebrated race in the English sporting calendar is the Derby Stakes run on Epsom Downs, some 17 miles south of London, normally on the first Wednesday in June, for three-year-old colts and fillies over a distance of 1 m 4 f. Colts carry 9 st and fillies (although they rarely run in the race it has been won by a filly on more than one occasion) carry 8 st 9 lb. The race gets its name from the 12th Earl of Derby and was decided by the toss of a coin with another of the turf's great patrons, Sir Charles Bunbury. Ironically, it was Sir Charles' colt Diomed, a distant relation of Troy, that won the first great race in 1780. This Blue Riband of the European turf was first run over 1 m and eventually extended to $1\frac{1}{2}$ m.

Epsom is a left-handed course $1\frac{1}{2}$ m in length. The track rises 150 ft in the first 4 f and falls 100 ft in varying gradients to the dip, with a considerable rise to the winning post. The world-famous Tattenham Corner is a long sweeping bend running downhill to the homestraight and the dip. The 6 f and 7 f tracks start on a spur. The sprint track which is straight is one of the fastest in Europe. Running across the downs is an unfenced extension of cross-country track which is used for the $2\frac{1}{4}$ m Great Metropolitan Handicap.

The Oaks is the major race of the season for three-year-old fillies. It is run over $1\frac{1}{2}$ m at the Epsom Summer meeting over the full Derby course and was first contested in 1779. The race got its name from the Earl of Derby's residence which was nearby and was won in 1779 by the filly Bridget, owned by the 12th Earl.

Newmarket
The once small East Anglian town of Newmarket surrounded by flat or rolling heathland has been the centre of British racing and breeding for centuries. Situated some 65 miles from London the centre was 'invented' in 1605 by James I, a keen hunting and hawking sportsman. Charles I continued the royal patronage but it was Charles II who really put Newmarket on the map in a big way. The merry Monarch's first official visit was in 1666 when he founded the Newmarket Town Plate, a race for amateur jockeys, male or female, still run today. Newmarket is the biggest centre for the training of racehorses in Great Britain.

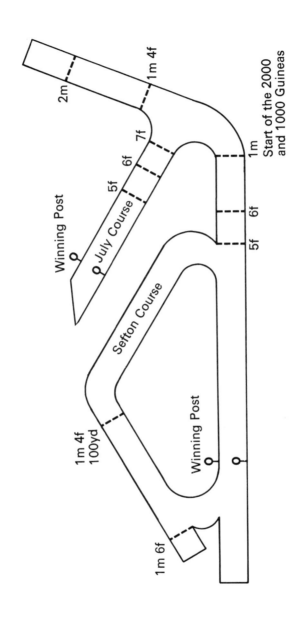

Newmarket Racecourse.

There are two racecourses on the heath. The Rowley Mile has a $1\frac{1}{4}$ m straight and stages the Cesarewitch Stakes over $2\frac{1}{4}$ m. Races of $1\frac{1}{2}$ m and upwards start beyond the Devils Dyke, an ancient earthworks, and bear right-handed into the straight at the $1\frac{1}{4}$ m start. The straight is fairly level until descending into 'The Dip' beside 'The Bushes', two famous landmarks at Newmarket, $2\frac{1}{2}$ f from the winning post. The final furlong is uphill and there are additional starts at $1\frac{3}{4}$ m, 1 m 4 f 100 yd, and $1\frac{1}{4}$ m. The July Course, used in June, July and August, has a straight mile, and races beyond that distance start on the Cesarewitch course, coming right-handed into the straight at the 1 m starting gate. The course is downhill from 6 f out until the final furlong which is uphill.

Two classic races, the 2,000 Guineas for three-year-old colts and fillies, first run in 1809, and the 1,000 Guineas for three-year-old fillies, first run in 1814, are staged over the straight Rowley Mile at the spring meeting. Towards the end of the season two famous handicaps, the Cesarewitch and the Cambridgeshire, known as the Autumn Double, and both established in 1839, are run at Newmarket. The Cesarewitch is a stayers' handicap run over $2\frac{1}{4}$ m and the Cambridgeshire a handicap run over a straight 1 m 1 f. Newmarket has always been one of the most important tracks at international racing level and the Champion Stakes run at the end of the flat-race season is one of the most vaulable races of the year. It was first run in 1877. The race is contested over $1\frac{1}{4}$ m and attracts the best international performers over that distance season after season.

York

York racecourse is often called the 'Ascot' of the North, although it stages only 15 days racing per year with the main meeting held in August. The course is level, well-drained and fitted with a modern watering system. York is a 'galloper's' track with sweeping bends providing a first-class test for good horses over any distance and in recent years has attracted runners from many parts of Europe.

Horse-racing in the district dates back to 1530 but the first record of racing on the present site, the Knavesmire, dates from 1731. The Knavesmire was originally a marsh for the grazing of commoners' cattle and is said to have been the site of the City gallows until 1802. York was a leading racecourse on the British circuit from its very beginnings but it did suffer a decline in the early part of the nineteenth century until, in 1843, a new clerk of the course, a certain Mr R. M. Jaques was appointed.

Mr Jaques brought a new era of prosperity and, while no classic

Horses from David Nicholson's Yard exercising.

race is run at York, the year 1843 saw the first running of one of the most important handicaps of the racing year, the Ebor Handicap raced over $1\frac{3}{4}$ m. The name of the race comes from Eboracum, the Roman name of the City of York.

But the Gimcrack Stakes is perhaps the most prestigious race staged at York. This is a 6 f 2-year-old race which often gives a very accurate form-pointer to the following season's classic races. The winning owner of the Gimcrack is, by tradition, the guest of honour and principal speaker at the Gimcrack dinner held in York later in the year.

The training centres in England tend to be situated near downland, moors or racecourses, many with long traditions like Lewes in Sussex, and Manton in Wiltshire where the great nineteenth century trainer John Porter had his stables and Malton, Yorkshire, from where John Scott, the first prominent public trainer on the English racing scene, turned out five Derby winners, nine Oaks' winners and no fewer than 16 St Leger winners between 1829 and 1863. Newmarket, Epsom, Lambourn and Malton are now the major racing centres in Britain. But many are now losing out to urban development with the tendency by new young trainers to set up at Newmarket, the nearest training grounds in England in style and layout to the European centralized centres. Newmarket trainer Henry Cecil headed the winning trainers list in 1980, winning 128 races and earning his patrons £683,971 in prize money.

The British National Stud was established in 1916 at Tully, County Kildare, Ireland, when Lord Wavertree gave his entire stud of bloodstock to the nation. At first it was Government sponsored. The stud was transferred from Ireland to Gillingham, Dorset in 1943 and was expanded in 1949 with the purchase of the West Grinstead Stud in Sussex. At that time the National stud had both brood mares and stallions and it was intended that the stud would breed racehorses good enough to stand as stallions. The best yearlings were for many years leased for their racing careers to the reigning monarch. The stud bred some very high-class horses, indeed, including Blandford, sire of four Derby winners, and the classic winners Big Game, Carrozza, Chamoisaire, Royal Lancer and Sun Chariot. In 1964 all the mares were sold and the stud policy was changed to the standing of stallions only.

In 1967 the National Stud was moved to its present home at Newmarket and although now without any State subsidization whatever it has been very successful in serving the bloodstock industry by retaining stallions that might otherwise have been exported for very large sums of money. The resident stallions at this point were a healthy mixture of sprinting blood, middle-distance blood and international bloodlines.

A very commercial admixture was supplied by the following horses: Blakeney, 1969 Derby winner; Mill Reef the ill-fated winner of the 1971 Derby; the game, tough Grundy 1975 Derby winner; Tudor Melody, a very successful stallion by Tudor Minstrel the 1947 2,000 Guineas winner and successful stallion in Europe and USA; the top-class miler Habat; and the German-trained 1975 Rix de l'Arc de Triomphe winner Star Appeal, sired by the Italian horse Appiani II, and reared in Ireland.

The National Stud's covering season is from February 15 through to July 15 and a visiting mare usually stays at the Stud until she is safely tested as in-foal, a period of about 14 weeks. Three and a half miles of road, 18 miles of fencing and some 40,000 trees make up the National Stud along with modern buildings accommodating the six stallions and, at any one time, about 200 brood mares. The Stud is open to the public on Sunday afternoons and Bank Holiday afternoons from April to June inclusive.

Ireland

England and Ireland, whatever their differences elsewhere, have always worked closely together in the Thoroughbred world. They share the same system of recording bloodlines, the *General Stud Book*, and Irish mares, originally kept on their own, have been recorded in the *GSB* since 1905. Ireland's record in the English classics has brought her breeding industry on a par with anywhere in the world. An industry it certainly is, for horse-racing in Ireland is more than a sport, it is almost a religion. There must be more horsemen and racing fans per lush green acre in the Emerald Isle than anywhere else in the world.

Although the boom in bloodstock sales came summarily to an end, which was not unexpected, in 1974, the products of Irish studs have more than held their own at the principal auction sales and on the racecourse since then in competition with Britain and other very much larger breeding and racing centres. The Republic of Ireland has probably the greatest density of recognized stud farms of any country in the world. The principal areas for large and smaller studs are concentrated in the Liffey Valley around Dublin, the Golden Vale of Tipperary and Kilkenny, and the Boyne Valley, which includes the prime counties of Meath and Kildare. Although large areas of the country consist of bog, mountain, forest and stony wasteland, the lush pastures of Ireland, rich in limestone and trace minerals, combined with a moist and agreeable climate, are ideal for the raising of sound, well-boned thoroughbred stock. At the same time, the notable success of imported American horses in recent years does suggest that Eire may not have that much advantage in natural resources.

There are some 370 stud farms in Ireland, covering some 70,000 statute acres and employing a total of about 4,000 people. In addition to the fully-fledged, highly capitalized studs largely owned by a small number of wealthy, internationally-orientated individuals or syndicates – of which the Killeen Castle Stud at Dunsany, Co. Meath, part of the Wildenstein breeding empire, is but one example – there has always been a considerable number of farmers and other individuals owning only one or two mares but who are not classified as studmasters. Santa Claus, Rheingold and Giocometti are three recent products of this kind of establishment which has unfortunately tended to disappear with the present economic conditions and recent changes in Irish tax laws.

In general, Ireland has a greater number of classic or top-grade stallions than Great Britain, and where there was only about a score of winners in Group I Pattern Races serving Ireland in the 1950's, that

53

number has now more than doubled. In all there are about 300 stallions in the country, including the outstandingly successful Red God, Whistler, Pall Mall, Royal Orbit and Sovereign Path, and about 4,700 brood mares. An enormous benefit to stallion owners and syndicates has been the introduction of the Irish Stallion Incentive Scheme, in operation since 1971, which pays bonuses to breeders of winners of certain major races. These include all races under both flat and jumping rules in Ireland, as well as places in the classic races, all classic and pattern races, and handicaps with £5,000 or more added to the stakes. Five major races in France were added in 1975.

Another advantage enjoyed by Irish stud owners is that covering fees for stallions are not subject to income tax, and livestock are not included in valuations for wealth tax.

Ireland has two entirely separate bloodstock auction centres, the Ballsbridge International Bloodstock Sales organization with its new £1.3 million Sales Centre in Dublin, and the century-old Goffs Sales which moved to a vast, luxurious sales complex at Kill in County Kildare in September, 1975. With no value added tax on bloodstock in Ireland, many leading British breeders prefer to sell their produce in Eire.

Although Ireland as an agricultural country tends to favour the breeder and producer, one area causing some concern to those involved in racing is the poor level of prize money. The average prize money per horse in training is less than £1,000 compared to some £6,814 in Japan (the highest figure of any country in the world). But many of the major races are now attracting commercial sponsorship so there is a trend upwards.

The Curragh, in the heart of Co. Kildare, is the headquarters of Irish racing. Eire's major training establishments are located around the wide, flat expanse of springy turf where sheep wander at will. The Curragh racecourse stages all five Irish classics and the majority of Ireland's semi-classic and Pattern races. The Irish Sweeps Derby, the first ever race in Ireland to top £100,000 in prize money and the Irish Guinness Oaks are the premier Irish Classics and attract runners from Britain and Europe.

Group I (Championship) Pattern races and major handicaps in Ireland have been dominated in recent years by the powerful stable of the 'wizard of Ballydoyle', Vincent O'Brien. The virtually unbeatable partnership of Vincent O'Brien and the great English jockey Lester Piggott has been largely based on the Tipperary stable's team of expensive American-bred horses. A quietly-spoken, slightly built figure, Vincent O'Brien, born in 1917, has an astounding record in major international races. He has won every classic race in England and Ireland, the Prix de l'Arc de Triomphe and the Washington International. Among the great horses trained by him have been Ballymoss, Sir Ivor, Gladness, Nijinsky and The Minstrel to name but a few. Vincent started out as a small trainer of point-to-pointers (Hunt racers) before taking out a full licence as a jumping trainer. He trained the winner of the important Cheltenham Gold Cup steeplechase three years in a row from 1948 to 1950 with Cottage Rake, the winner of the Champion Hurdle, Hattons Grace, in 1949, 1950 and 1951 and the world-famous Grand National steeplechase in three consecutive years with three different steeplechasers. He is one of a small select band of British trainers to produce the winners of both the Grand National and the Derby.

Another Irish training 'giant' is the colourful Paddy Prendagast whose Meadow Court stable has sent out the winners of practically every important race in England and Ireland. These include English 2,000 Guineas winner Martial (1960), Epsom Derby runner-up and Irish Derby winner Meadow Court (1965) and English St Leger winner Ragusa.

If the Curragh is Ireland's international shop-window and the only course likely to attract the cream of international runners because of the low level of prize money outside the classic programme, the domestic racing scene has plenty to offer the Irish racegoer in both quaint charm and sophistication. Leopardstown, set against the background of the Wicklow Mountains, has superb modern facilities for both flat and jump-racing. Although the flat programme tends to be overshadowed by the Curragh, a cause for complaint among many of its supporters, Leopardstown comes into its own during the winter when all the major steeplechase and hurdle prestige races except the Irish Grand National staged at Fairyhouse, are held, including the valuable Leopradstown Chase, invariably an accurate pointer to England's Cheltenham Gold Cup. Past winners include the fabulous Arkle.

Phoenix Park, in the heart of Dublin city, is another chic track which regularly attracts huge crowds from the Irish capital and abroad, while those who enjoy a truly 'Irish' race-meeting, with all the informality and lack of inhibition that goes with it, cross the country for Galway races, or drive down to Killarney and Tranmore where the twisting, slightly less than level tracks often provide the most startling results!

P. Gunn, on rails, wins the Thames Selling Handicap Stakes at Kempton.

4
Racing in North America

The vast size of the North American continent is one of the chief reasons why racing there is based on a pattern of Regional Racing Boards and State Circuits as against the more straight forward organization of a national circuit under one Jockey Club or Rules of Racing Board, as in Britain for example. The two major circuits are on the western and eastern seaboards; New York is the senior centre of the east and the Californian tracks of Santa Anita and Hollywood Park are the major centres of the west.

Centralized control, in comparison with Europe, is relatively

Diomed won the first running of the English Derby in 1780 and later came to the USA where he sired many thoroughbreds. From a rare old painting by courtesy of the Parker Gallery, London.

weakened by the independence of State Racing Commissions, hundreds of track associations and the immense size of the racing industry. But the advantage of this is to create a far greater competitive atmosphere between owners, trainers and breeders. This is particularly true of the breeders, who run highly commercial stud farms, raising stock directly for the sales rings. Breeders in one area try a great deal harder when they know that their stock must outshine the stock of another state if they are to stay in business. This natural love of free enterprise has created one of the most powerful racehorse breeding countries in the world.

Thoroughbred racing is by far the biggest spectator sport in the USA and the courses are highly geared to the betting public with attendances totalling about 50 million people annually. The tracks are oval or circular with dirt, tan, sand or grass surfaces and the total value of stud farms, racetracks and horses was estimated recently at five billion dollars.

Although the horse tends to be more a number than a name to the average racegoer, the successful ones are treated with a fan-worship equal to that of any Hollywood film idol. Some of the great ones of the past that have been bedecked with laurels, tributes and hero-worship were the legendary Man O'War or 'Big Red', the 1948 Triple Crown winner Citation, and Buckpasser, a magnificent colt who won his owner Ogden Phipps a total of $1,462,000 in just three years of racing between 1975 and 1977. Buckpasser retired to stud with a racing record of 31 starts and 25 wins. Other great ones are Secretariat, winner of $1,316,808 including the American Triple Crown (the first since Citation 25 years earlier), Seatle Slew and the 1978 Triple Crown winner Affirmed who amassed an incredible $2.1 million in prize money. Affirmed went on to race as a 4-year-old and became the most valuable horse ever when he was syndicated for $14.4 million. The colt is now at stud on the Spendthrift Farm.

The atmosphere of North American racing is totally different to the staid and often fanciful air of British racecourses. Early in the morning on race-days the horses are worked on the track. Later when racing starts the horses are paraded in the paddock, race-programmes and 'handicap' sheets supply the race-fan with complete track record information and training work-out results on each runner. The Pari-Mutuel odds-board, a mosaic of flashing lights and digits with a periodic flash of 'Welcome to the Hackensack Elks', gives an instant read-out of the betting market and the exotic landscaping of the infield, on one track inhabited by pink flamingos, are all part of the beauty and colour of an American race-day. The runners for each race

59

Man O'War winning the Jockey Club Gold Cup, 1920.

are paraded in front of the grandstand before being 'ponied' (led) down to the starting gates by a liveried mounted escort. More emphasis is put on the entertainment and betting aspects of thoroughbred racing. The average race programme, which can vary from 8 to 10 races, tends to have more claiming races than in Europe. Claiming races are, in fact, selling races, an owner, trainer or racing manager enters a horse in a claimer with his 'value'. For example, if a horse is entered with a claiming price of say $5,000, then that horse can be claimed, in effect purchased, for $5,000. In a selling race, however, the winner, and sometimes the second and third, are auctioned after the race. In North America and Europe, these races are often a good way for a first-time racehorse owner to acquire a racehorse that wins him a few minor races but the selling race in

THE WINNER OF THE DERBY RACE.

1 The course and grandstand at Epsom in 1836.

2 Rowlandson's caricature of Dr Syntax at the York Races, dated 1815.

DOCTOR SYNTAX
LOSING HIS MONEY ON THE RACE GROUND AT YORK.

Drawn & Etched by H. Alken Esq.

ASCOT RACES. *Tom & Bob win*.

London Pub.

3 Early nineteenth century print by Henry Alkan showing racing at Ascot.

…e long odds from a knowing one.

…ine 22nd 1822.

4 *Vanity Fair* cartoon of Admiral the Hon. Henry John Rous (1795-1877) one of the 'great dictators' of turf history.

5 Richard Tattersall (1724-1795) one of the first dealers in racehorses, founder of Tattersalls.

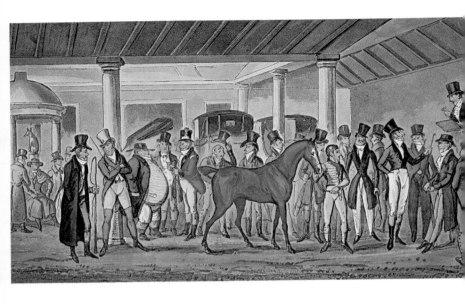

6 A George Cruikshank cartoon of a horse auction at Tattersalls.

7 Print showing Gladiateur, the famous French horse, at Epsom in 1865.

8 Start at Longchamp, Paris.

9 Starting stalls at Aqueduct Racecourse, New York.

10 The crack French racemare Allez-France, with Yves St Martin in the saddle. They won the 1974 Grand Prix de l'Arc de Triomphe.

11 Secretariat, record-breaking winner of the USA Triple Crown in 1973, at the Claiborne Farm, Kentucky where he is at stud.

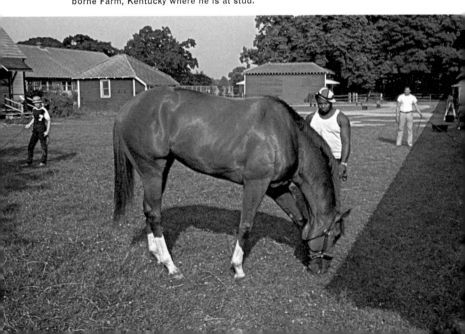

12 Brigadier Gerard, British Classic winner, ridden by Joe Mercer.

13 Grundy, Epsom Derby winner in 1975, now at the National Stud at Newmarket.

14 Epsom on Derby Day.

15 In the paddock at Newmarket racecourse.

16 A crowded grandstand at Ascot.

17 Formal dress at Royal Ascot.

18 Going out to the paddock at Epsom races. Pat Eddery talks to Brian Taylor, with John Reid behind them in the centre.

19 Vincent O'Brien, the international trainer (centre) studies The Derby from the Epsom rails with racehorse owners Mr and Mrs Robert Sangster (left).

20 The Royal Ascot judges in full morning dress.

21 Lester Piggott (light and dark green) and Joe Mercer (red and white stripes), both champion British jockeys, leave the starting stalls at Newbury.

22 A finish at Newmarket races with Lorelene (No. 15) and H.M. the Queen's Restful (No. 27), ridden by British champion jockey Willie Carson.

23 George Moore (No. 4), the great Australian jockey, leads the field at Newmarket races.

24 Runners bunch up close as they take an Ascot bend.

25 The French-trained Nureyev (Philippe Pacquet up) passes the post first in the 1980 2,000 Guineas at Newmarket. After a Steward's Inquiry, Known Fact, the English-trained colt (in sheepskin noseband), ridden by Willie Carson, was declared the winner.

26 Kris (Joe Mercer) winning the 1979 Bisquit Cognac Stakes.

27 Pawnese (Yves St Martin) winning the Oaks in 1976.

28 Henbit, ridden by Willie Carson (red spots), storms up the hill to win the 1980 Epsom Derby from Master Willie (Philip Waldron – red sleeves).

29 Henbit (American-bred), owned by Mrs Etty Plesch, in the winner's enclosure. It was soon realized that the colt had a crack in his off-fore cannon-bone.

30 Tyrnavos (Edward Hide) winning the Ascot Heath Stakes.

31 Shirley Heights (Greville Starkey) wins the 1978 Epsom Derby from Hawaian Sound (Willie Shoemaker).

32 Bookies at Brighton racecourse.

33 Handlers load a runner into the starting stalls at Sandown Park.

34 Bireme, daughter of Grundy and 1980 Oaks winner, owned by R. Hollingsworth, comes up the rails under Willie Carson to take the Musidora Stakes at York.

35 View of the parade ring and grandstand at York.

36 Horses from Peter Walwyn's training stables at Lambourn on the gallop.

37 Relaxing on the way home after exercise.

38 Going down the backstretch on Preakness Day at Pimlico Racetrack, Baltimore, USA.

39 The 'big star' treatment for a classic colt in the winner's enclosure at Pimlico racetrack after the Preakness Stakes, the second leg of the US Triple Crown.

40 Racing down the backstretch at Aqueduct Racecourse, Long Island, New York State.

41 New York – Meadowland. Neptune at the finish under floodlights.

42 Grandstand crowd at Longchamp, Paris.

43 At the paddock rails, Longchamp, Paris.

44 Mill Reef (owned by Mr Paul Mellon) and Geoff Lewis being led in after winning the 1971 Grand Prix de l'Arc de Triomphe at Longchamp.

45 Going for the winning post at Longchamp.

46 The charming Chantilly racecourse, just outside Paris, with the old stables on the left, and the *château* in the background.

47 Racing in the South of France.

48 The winner's enclosure at Deauville racecourse, France.

49 Exercising horses on the beach at Deauville.

50 Dahlia (left), with Australian jockey Bill Pyers, canters down to the start at Longchamp.

51 Star Appeal (Greville Starkey) wins the 1975 Grand Prix de l'Arc de Triomphe.

52 The German-trained Star Appeal gets a pat after the race from Frau Waldemar Zeitelhack.

53 From left to right: Yves St Martin, the Aga Khan, François Mathet.

54 Maisons Laffitte training stables.

55 Alleged (Lester Piggott) wins the 1978 'Arc' from Tricolor.

56 Three Troikas (Freddie Head) wins the 1979 Grand Prix de l'Arc de Triomphe.

57 Country Race Meeting, Wellington, N.S.W.

58 Racehorses parading before Australia's top race – the Melbourne Cup at Flemington.

59 The finish at Happy Valley, Hong Kong.

60 The fabulous Sha Tin racecourse, Hong Kong, with its large video screen showing a close-up of the races as they are run.

61 Grandstand at Happy Valley, Hong Kong.

62 Coming round the final bend at Happy Valley, Hong Kong.

63 Weighing room at Sha Tin, Hong Kong. Top UK jockey, Geoff Lewis is standing in the background on the right.

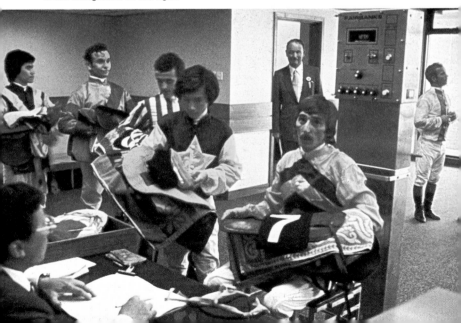

64 Willie Shoemaker, USA.

65 Steve Cauthen, from Kentucky, USA, now based in Europe.

66 Yves St Martin, France, idolized by the French racing public.

67 Philippe Pacquet, France, a crack apprentice who has become a leading international jockey.

68 Lester Piggott, UK, one of the finest jockeys Britain has produced.

69 Betting in the summer rain at Chester racecourse, UK.

England and Ireland is best left to the experts. Handicaps, too, figure more in race programmes than the popular European condition or weight-for-age races.

It was not until the beginning of this century that the American Thoroughbred really started to make his mark in the world. His journey to the top was a typical American success story where to be the best he got out and beat the best. For two forms of legislation, designed to cripple American racing and thoroughbred breeding, in fact, did quite the opposite. The European 'Jersey Act' and the US anti-betting motions, as it turns out, were perhaps the best blessings in disguise the sport could have had. Never have the ashes of disaster become the roses of success with such penetrating results.

The 'Jersey Act' forced North American breeders to become more selective in breeding policies and marketing by concentrating on building blood-lines with direct relation to track performances rather than producing fashionable stallions. After the Civil War racing became a major public leisure activity with betting and bookmakers the main attraction. Over the years new racetracks opened all over the Union, race-meetings became longer and longer, inter-track rivalry became almost a gang-warfare, racing promoters and racehorse owners were at odds with State and local politicians, and transgressions by bookmakers were predominant. The racing game and its followers were not all that popular or trusted by other members of the community. A great deal of public support built up in many states for the banning of betting on horseraces. Many states brought in anti-betting laws until by 1908 the number of racetracks in the USA had fallen from 314 to 25 and in Canada from 43 to 6! But worse was to come for in 1910 the State of New York passed a law banning all betting and making its racetracks responsible for the enactment of the law. The bookmakers of the turn-of-the-century used to stand on the lawns of the Empire City Racetrack, with their 'sheet-writers' recording each wager before disappearing or going underground. No money changed hands as betting was done on credit, with accounts settled at the end of the day, week or month depending on the individual arrangement. The end result was a two-year suspension of racing in New York, the home of the Jockey Club which was at that time the ruling body of American racing.

Today the powers of the Jockey Club have been transferred to the State Racing Commissions and the Thoroughbred Racing Authority (T.R.A.) while the Jockey Club maintains the integrity of the stud Book and acts as adviser to the racing boards.

On May 30, 1913 the New York track at Belmont Park re-opened its gates with legal and licensed bookmakers but the feelings of the anti-betting legislation were still there and gradually one state after another outlawed bookmakers and permitted their racetracks to install pari-mutuel machines (totalisator). The state treasuries took, through a tax levy, a percentage of the pari-mutuel pool which could be put to the benefit of everybody and the racetrack management was able to make a healthy profit and increase prize money. By this means the state government gained a vested interest in racing and the high prize money encouraged sportsmen to own racehorses and breeders to invest larger sums in bloodstock. So thanks to what might seem rather puritanical laws today the future prosperity of American horse-racing and bloodstock breeding was laid.

Kentucky has long been the most famous region in the United States devoted to the production of thoroughbreds but in recent times it has had to fend off challenges from California, Virginia, Florida and Pennsylvania. It is in Kentucky, the Blue Grass Country, that some of the most famous and successful stud farms in the world are found, like Claiborne, Spendthrift, Gainesway and the Bluegrass Farm.

In Kentucky, too, are a great many farms devoted entirely to the raising of Standardbred horses for harness racing – trotting and pacing. There are others on which the American Quarter Horse is bred. These tremendously fast sprinting horses have their own racing circuits. The All-American Futurity, a championship race for Quarter Horses run over 440 yd at Ruidoso Downs, New Mexico, is worth a world-record total prize money of $1,280,000. The 1978 the winner Moon Lark collected a world-record $437,500 first prize.

The celebrated Blue Grass State of Kentucky is the area within a 25-mile radius of the centre of the city of Lexingtion. The Thoroughbred Breeders' Association of Kentucky produced in 1976 a survey showing 414 thoroughbred stud farms in the state, with 75% of them in the Blue Grass country. The farms range from 10 acres to the 6,000 acres each which make up the spreads of the Claiborne Stud and the Spendthrift Stud.

The resident team of stallions at Claiborne Farm has averaged about 25 in recent years and their names read like an equine 'Who's Who': Secretariat, winner of the American Triple Crown (Kentucky Derby, Preakness Stakes and Belmont Stakes); Nijinsky, the English Triple Crown winner; Sir Ivor, the English Derby winner; and Buckpasser and Latin-American-bred Damascus, both of whom earned the title Horse of the Year in their racing days on American tracks. Claiborne employs nearly 200 staff and can accommodate some 450 mares in the breeding season.

110

Spendthrift Farm was the home of Mill Reef's sire, Never Bend. Stallion residents now include Majestic Prince – winner of the Kentucky Derby and Preakness Stakes, Wajima – the 1973 3-year-old champion of the USA and Affirmed, 1979's wonder-horse, winner of the 1978 American Triple Crown. There are some 22 resident stallions at Gainesway farm including the English Derby winner Empery and his sire Vaguely Noble, winner of the 1968 Prix de l'Arc de Triomphe and whose progeny includes the record-breaking racemare Dahlia.

Many American states and provinces of Canada are now establishing thoroughbred breeding centres. The western state of California is actually slightly ahead of Kentucky in number of foals produced per annum. Swaps and Decidedly, both winners of the Kentucky Derby, were raised in the semi-desert conditions of California where the young stock are fed like horses in training from weaning onwards. Mrs Penny and Known Fact, both important winners in England during the 1979 season were not bred in Kentucky. Mrs Penny was bred at Marshall Jenney's Derry Meeting Farm in Pennsylvania which produces some 450 foals per year and Known Fact was bred in the south-eastern State of Florida by veterinarian Dr William Read at the Mare Haven Farm near Ocala. The state of Florida has climbed rapidly up the North American bloodstock league for less than 25 years ago there was no breeding industry in the state but it is now the third biggest thoroughbred producer behind California and Kentucky. For quality as well as quantity Florida rates highly, too, having produced four Kentucky Derby winners including the equine superstar Affirmed.

All-powerful as it is in the bloodstock markets of the world, Kentucky remembers the past and in a quiet corner of the Claiborne estate is a stallions' cemetery – a line of graves each with its own headstone on which is carved the names of former residents of the stallion barns, some of the most renowned in American and International Turf history. Sir Gallahad III, a French-bred horse that won the English Lincolnshire handicap as a four-year-old before going to Kentucky, where he bred three winners of the Kentucky Derby, is buried there. Kentucky Derby winners Johnstown and Gallant Fox lie there along with the late Aga Khan's 'gift-horses' to the American industry, Blenheim and Nassrullah. Princequillo, sire of the great Round Table, and Court Martial, winner of the 1945 English 2,000gns and who died at Claiborne in his 24th year, have adjoining plots, and Secretariat's sire Bold Ruler is also buried there.

Kentucky, quite rightly, boasts another popular horse-memorial at Man O'War Park in Fayette County. Here a bronze statue, one and a quarter times life size, of the legendary 'Big Red' stands looking out over the lush rolling hills of the Blue Grass Country. Man O'War won the Preakness Stakes and the Belmont Stakes, two legs of the American Triple Crown, in 1920.

Racecourses

The majority of the racecourses in the USA have the same type of dirt or tan racing surface – ideal for centralized racing and training. Most of the trainers take one or two horse-barns at the racetrack to house their strings for the duration of the meeting which is often some 8 to 10 weeks. Most of the training is done on the tracks but many of the leading trainers and stud farms have home-based training centres which are laid out on practically the same pattern as the race-tracks.

With a few exceptions the American trainer, unlike his European colleagues, trains his horses to the clock. With most of the American racecourses uniform in shape and flat, he must train his horses to run ... and run fast. The runners leave the starting stalls much quicker than in Europe, encouraged by the flatness of the racestrip and the eveness of the ground. There are also more sprint races This means that the horse must find his racing stride almost immediately after leaving the stalls.

Further, as all the courses are oval with short home-stretches, it is vital to secure a good position early in order to find the shortest way home. All fast work and trials, which in American terms can mean a 'gallop' or a 'breeze' which is a harder, faster work-out than a gallop, are clocked by the trainer. He will have at his fingertips the average times for certain distances at the tracks ... the fastest times and the slowest. So the American racehorse is from the first trained to race against the clock. In a trial, that would be a training spin at racing pace, the horse is matched against horses whose track-times are known by the trainer and he can relate the performance to the standard of competition his horse is going to face.

The leading trainers have large strings and are under far more pressure from their patrons than their European colleagues. The American racehorse is expected to live up to his name and race. The trainer is allotted a barn or stalls at the track and the racecourse authorities expect him to run each horse he takes.

Racing is an all-year round sport in North America. The New York circuit is almost year-round; the Californian season runs from late December through to the following October; the Florida circuit runs from mid-November through to April and there are busy race-circuits

Aqueduct Racecourse.

in Maryland, Kentucky, New Jersey, Illinois, New England, New Mexico and Delaware. So, have racehorse – will travel, is almost a password in America.

Aqueduct

Like Belmont Park and Saratoga Park, Aqueduct is administered by the New York Racing Association and attracts nearly $4\frac{1}{2}$ million racegoers each year. It is predominately a 'speed' track with a very large grandstand which runs parallel to the long home-stretch. The racing surface is sand with wide, even turns.

Many important races are staged at Aqueduct, but perhaps the best known are the Suburban Handicap and the Brooklyn Handicap both run in July and framed for 3-year-olds and upwards. The Suburban is run over $1\frac{3}{8}$ m and the Brooklyn over $1\frac{2}{8}$ m.

Belmont Park

Belmont Park was named after August Belmont, a renowned banker and Racehorse owner. The track opened in 1905 but in 1911–12 New York racing was suspended through anti-betting legislation which eventually led to the outlawing of bookmakers. Belmont opened its gates again in 1913 and in 1968 the 'new' Belmont was opened boasting the world's largest grandstand at a cost of $30,700,000. The new stand is 110 ft high, 440 yd long, contains 908 pari-mutuel windows and seats 30,000 racegoers. Like Aqueduct, Belmont Park, New Jersey, NY, has a sand racing surface and is predominately a speed track.

Belmont Park is the home of the Belmont Stakes, senior of the three American classics for colts and first run in 1867 at Jerome Park, now closed, then at Morris Park from 1890 until settling at Belmont Park in 1905. The race has been contested over various distances starting at $1\frac{5}{8}$ m from 1867 until 1873 until the present distance of $1\frac{1}{2}$ m was established in 1926.

The first British-bred winner was Saxon in 1874; the immortal Man O'War won it in 1920. Also staged at Belmont Park is the Coaching Club American Oaks. This race is to 3-year-old fillies what the 'Belmont' is for colts, and with the Acorn Stakes and the Mother Goose Stakes, makes up the ladies' Triple Crown.

Churchill Downs

Churchill Downs, in the heart of the Blue Grass Country, is to American racing what Epsom is to English racing and Longchamp is to the French turf. Churchill Downs, home of the Kentucky Derby,

Churchill Downs, Derby Day, 1941.

Swaps winning the Kentucky Derby, 1955.

runs two seasons – one from late April to late May, and the other from early September to early October. It is a 1 m oval shaped track with very sharp bends and a long 1,234 ft homestraight. It is a very fast track which favours speed horses.

The Kentucky Derby was first run over the course in 1875 at the distance of $1\frac{2}{8}$ m Although in its long career the race has been contested over $1\frac{1}{2}$ m, it finally settled at it present distance of $1\frac{2}{8}$ m in 1896. The first winner was Aristides, and the first horse foaled outside the USA to win the Kentucky Derby was the British horse Omar Khayyan in 1917 – the year that another British-bred horse, Hourless, won the Belmont Stakes.

The great Man O'War did not run in the Kentucky Derby, but his son, War Admiral, won the race in 1937 on his way to landing the Triple Crown. Since its inauguration, the race has been dominated by Kentucky-bred horses, though in recent years this monopoly has been dented on more than one occasion. Swaps (1955) was the first Californian-bred horse to win it, beating the locally-bred favourite Nashua. In 1964 Northern Dancer brought the spotlight on the Canadian horse, winning the Kentucky Derby and the Preakness Stakes and, in 1978, Affirmed did the same for the Pennsylvanian-bred racehorse by taking the 'Derby' and the Triple Crown.

Native Dancer winning the Wood Memorial, 1953.

117

Racing starts at Pimlico, Baltimore, near Maryland, in early March and runs into late May. The track has a 1 m main oval track with a $\frac{7}{8}$ m grass course inside it. The racing surface at Pimlico is deep and soft favouring horses that come-from-behind to win their races although, usually, the track is skimmed and made harder in order to establish a fast time for the track's top stakes event, the Preakness. Pimlico, with its 1,152 ft homestretch, is one of the oldest racecourses in America and the home of the Preakness Stakes, one third of the American Triple Crown classic title, first run there in 1873. The Preakness has had a chequered career, involving changes of distance, a four-year abandonment and some changes of venue. It was run at Pimlico until 1889 during which time the distance had been reduced from $1\frac{1}{2}$ m to $1\frac{2}{8}$ m, and was then abandoned until 1893. In 1894, the race was revived at Gravesend, New York, when the winner was Assignee. Then in 1909 the Preakness returned to Pimlico as a mile race but its present distance of $9\frac{1}{2}$ f was adopted in 1925 when the race went to a horse called Coventry.

Many great American horses have won the Preakness. The legendary Man O'War, the flying Triple Crown winner Citation, Bold Ruler, Native Dancer, Canada's Northern Dancer and 1979's most valuable horse ever, Affirmed.

Laurel Park
Maryland racing moves to Laurel Park, Washington D.C., from late October through December. The Laurel main track is $1\frac{1}{8}$ m around and the turf course, a very good one, measures 1 mile. The turns are sweeping and the track surface is deep and slow. The Laurel management follow the policy to forsake speed in preference to the horses running on their track remaining sound after racing. Laurel Park is the scene of the Washington International invitation race, a turf event over $1\frac{1}{2}$ m and now one of the most important races in America. The race, first run in 1952, was the brainchild of the President of Laurel Park, John D. Schapiro, who travels the world promoting the race and looking for horses to invite. These normally go out to winners of Group 1 Pattern Races in Europe, the Emperor's Cup in Japan and the State Cup races in Australia.

The Australian horse Sailor's Guide won the 'Laurel' in 1958, after the disqualification of the English-bred Tudor Era. Hawaii, a horse that came from South Africa although trained in the USA at the time, was runner-up in 1969 to the English winner Karabas. Further proof of the 'Laurel's' international rating has been the appearance of

Russian racehorses in Maryland. Two of Russia's best racehorses, Zabeg and Anilin, measured up well to top-class international form. In 1960 Zabeg was third behind the American horses Bald Eagle and Hormonizing and finished a creditable fourth the following two years. Anilin, a winner of 22 races from 28 starts in six countries, was third in 1964 to the top American stakes winners Kelso and Gun Bow, and in 1966 Anilin, three times winner of the Grosser Preis von Europa, West Germany's richest race, finished second to Behistoun.

5
Racing in Europe

Flat-racing is enjoyed in most parts of Europe, Sweden, Denmark, Norway, Holland, Belgium, France, Switzerland, Italy and West Germany, with each country running its own centralized form of organization and most of them operating a Tote monopoly betting system. The pattern of racing is largely modelled on the English version with a series of three-year-old's classic races, Derby and St Leger etc, and championship races for the four-year-olds and upwards.

France

The super-power of European racing is France, where it is rare for horses, trainers and jockeys to travel from one end of the country to the other for a race meeting, as they do, for example, in Britain and to a lesser extent in the USA. When organized racing was started in France in 1834, the French were able to start, as it were, from 'zero-plus', and take advantage of the centuries of pioneering that had already been spent by English breeders in trying to produce a clean-bred racehorse.

Because of the size of the country, the style of racing in France has always been centralized around the most densely populated regions. The largest of these is Paris which, by the mere nature of its position, is the top-end of the sport in France. There are two main training centres: at Chantilly and Maisons Laffitte. Race meetings are held regularly at Longchamp and St Cloud in the city of Paris, and at Chantilly, Maisons Laffitte and Evry which are just outside the metropolis. So there is very little travelling involved for the runners and their handlers.

This routine only changes during August, the *mois des vacances* for the Parisians, when nearly all the leading strings emigrate to Deauville for five solid weeks of racing by the seaside.

The race card usually consists of six to seven races which will normally include a race restricted to apprentice jockeys, or amateurs or *amazones* (lady-riders), a selling race (*à réclamer*), a handicap, and condition races for two-year-olds and three-year-olds. The French pattern of races (a series of valuable races framed to test and discover the best horses of all ages) has for some time now put its emphasis on races from one mile to two miles with little emphasis on sprinters. This has tended to direct their breeding industry towards producing good three-year-olds rather than sharp and speedy two-year-olds that do not train on, or do not go on, to their three-year-old seasons with any capabilities beyond six furlongs. French successes in classic races, especially in England, and Group I championship pattern races since World War II have proved the wisdom of this system of framing races.

Bookmaking became illegal by a law of 1891 and from then on all betting was confined to Pari-Mutuels operated by the racecourse companies. By the same law, the racecourse companies were made non-profit making bodies and compelled to utilize their resources for the improvement of racing and racehorses. This has brought, besides a hefty source of income for the national treasury, increasing benefits to the sport and produced racecourses that are superbly looked after, with amenties like restaurants, bars, childrens' playgrounds, betting halls and landscaped gardens, which are second to none.

The vast resources available from the PMU have also helped to create a healthy industry for those involved in the sport by way of substantial prize-money and premiums to breeders. While a considerable percentage has gone into creating the training centres at Chantilly and Maisons Laffitte and the apprentice schools.

Chantilly, a few kilometres outside the city limits, is the Newmarket of France. On entering the town the signpost reads, Chantilly, Cité du Cheval – and that is exactly what it is. All the cafés and hotels carry names connected with racing, like Le Jockey Club and Bar des Lads, and along most of the roads runs a narrow sand-strip for the strings of racehorses to use on their way to the training grounds. The stable yards, some of them capable of housing well over a hundred thoroughbreds, are dotted around the main town or its neighbour Lamorlaye, within easy reach of the training areas.

The training facilities are among the best in the world with sand-canters and gallops, tree-lined gallops, well protected exercise rings, practice starting stalls, schooling fences, railed gallops in the forest and lush green strips for fast trials and pre-race gallops. Three areas of differing geophysical adavantages make up the training grounds, one at the Piste des Aigles near the main town, one at Lamorlaye on the road to Paris, and the other in the Forest of Chantilly near the *château* and the racecourse.

The Piste des Aigles is similar to the training grounds at

Newmarket, a vast open area of expertly maintained grassland with small clumps of trees where the strings can walk around to cool off after work or where the trainers, jockeys and work-riders can organize their morning's work schedules. Around the perimeter are sanded tree-lined rides where the racehorses can be limbered up before a fast work-out or calmly 'hacked around' to cool off before returning home.

The grass gallops are marked out with small gorse bushes and each strip is moved on a regular rotation system so that the ground is protected. In summer, watering systems are used during the dry months to keep the 'going' in perfect order and suitable for fast work.

At Lamorlaye, the training grounds run alongside the main Paris road. They are completely enclosed by white railings. The outer perimeter, which is mainly used for steady work, is a circular sand gallop enclosed by tall trees and railings similar to those seen on a racecourse. Around the track, entrances are marked 500 m, 800 m, 1,000 m and so on, so that trainers can give precise instructions to their lads on how far they want their charges to be worked. Within this perimeter is a network of walking, trotting and cantering sand-tracks and tree-covered areas for walking strings round. Beyond the perimeter are grass gallops mainly used for two-year-olds and year-lings, and practice starting stalls.

Maisons Laffitte, although not quite as vast as the training grounds at Chantilly, offers more or less the same facilities. The big difference is that it is actually a suburb of Paris and that of the few steeple-chasers and hurdlers trained in Paris, the best ones tend to be produced by the Maisons Laffitte stables.

Outside Paris, the next big centre is Marseilles, with Lyons a very close third. In Marseilles, the training grounds and stable yards are centred around the racecourse of Parc Borely in the seaside suburb of Bonneveinne. Here the set-up is quite different to Paris. The training gallop is set inside the circular racecourse and is narrow sand-track. The trotting track, a hard sand-coloured surface, is used for general exercising and in the middle of it all are the schooling fences and practice starting stalls. The racecourse, along with the course at Pont de Vivaux, is often used for fast work and trial gallops.

The French Thoroughbred

The French Thoroughbred, known as the *Pur-Sang Anglais*, as distinct from other clean-bred native breeds, has evolved as one of the best racehorses in the world. This is particularly apparent at the middle distances from 1,600 m to 3,000 m. The *Pur-Sang Anglais* was

Pawnese, winner of the 1976 Oaks and King George VI and Queen Elizabeth Stakes.

originally created in the mid-nineteenth century from stock imported from England. In latter years, some of the more powerful breeders like Marcel Boussac, François Dupré, Edmond Blanc, Alexandre Aumont, Comte Frederick de Lagrange, Jean Stern and the Rothschild family have invested heavily and shrewdly in the bloodstock industry and have been directly instrumental in bringing its production to international standards.

But the most important thing these breeders did for the French racehorse – they were all very successful businessmen having made their fortunes in such areas as mining and textiles – was to create stud farms and private training establishments so that their carefully planned produce could be followed through to the real test on the racecourse, as against stock reared for the yearling sales. This way they could follow a breeding line through, record its racing ability, and then decide where and when to in-breed or outcross that line in order to improve it. In the case of a very successful line that produced

123

a classic winner they could bring it back to the home stud to mantain the strain.

After World War II the French racehorse really started to make its mark internationally, with regular successful raids on the English classics as well as beating some of the best European horses on their home ground – the Paris racetracks. Then in the 1960's a strong injection of American racing blood was brought into the French thoroughbred with the result that today, after more than a century, it can take its place in international racing and looks like staying right up at the top for many years to come.

Racecourses

Chantilly

This racecourse is sited on a 60 hectare open park area between the small, but charming *château* and the main *Route Nationale* which runs through the town. The Forest of Chantilly, with its network of sand and grass rides and training gallops, borders the back of the grandstand and paddock. The surface is grass, with a round course, a horse-shoe shaped course and a straight track.

In the early 1830's Chantilly supplemented and eventually replaced the racecourse in the Champ de Mars in Paris, where French flat-racing first started in 1834. It is the home of two French classics the Prix du Jockey Club (French Derby) and the Prix de Diane (French Oaks). The Prix du Jockey Club, founded in 1836, is run over 2400 m. Horses owned by Lord Henry Seymour, the 'Admiral Rous' of the French Turf, won the 'Derby' four times. The last of these was Poetess in 1841, sired by Lord Seymour's imported English stallion Royal Oak, which became one of the greatest broodmares in France. Eleven winners of the race have come from the Haras de Fresnay-le-Buffard, the property of one of France's most influential post World War II owners and breeders, Marcel Boussac, ex-President of the Société d'Encouragement. The French Derby is run on the second Sunday in June and the Prix de Diane, for 3-year-old fillies, is staged on the first Sunday in June over a distance of 2,100 m.

The French Jockey Club, mainly a social club, was founded in 1883. But the Société d'Encouragement pour l'Amelioration des Races de Chevaux en France (better known as the Société d'Encouragement) controls racing throughout France and administers the racecourses at Chantilly, Longchamp and Deauville. The Société was founded on November II, 1833 and in its manifesto of March 16, 1834, it declared its aim to improve the breeding strains in France by introducing pure thoroughbred blood – mainly English, hence the title *Pur-Sang Anglais*.

Longchamp

The idea of creating a major racecourse in the exquisite parkland of the Bois de Boulogne in the very heart of Paris is said to have been thought up by the Emperor Napoleon III. The Emperor, along with his friend the sucessful owner/breeder Comte Frederic de Lagrange, was keen to establish a racecourse and a race that would attract a bigger public to racing and contribute towards encouraging breeders to produce horses of quality and stamina. So from its opening the Emperor was proved right, for the course staged its first meeting in April 1857 and brought a new prosperity to racing and a new classic race.This was the Grand Prix de Paris, first run in 1863 and framed for three-year-old colts and fillies. The Grand Prix de Paris is equivalent to the British St Leger within the classic format of three-year-old racing. But as a race of 3,200 m it is a tougher test for staying thoroughbreds as its is run much earlier in the season at the end of June whereas the British St Leger comes much later in a three-year-olds 'classic' season being run in the autumn. The first winner of the Grand Prix de Paris was, ironically, a British horse called The Ranger.

Standing just inside the elegant iron entrance gates to Lonchamp stands a noble statue of Gladiateur, one of the greatest racehorses ever produced in France, if not in the world. The 'Avenger of Waterloo' won the British Triple Crown and the Grand Prix de Paris in 1865 and is said to have won the Ascot Gold Cup in England in 1866 by an incredible 40 lengths!

The course was modernized in 1966, when new stands were built with elevators to take racegoers up to their boxes or to the members' stand. New restaurants, bars, weighing room, offices etc, were sited around the landscaped lawns behind the immense grandstand. The paddock is one of the most attractive in the world, and on big-race days, its immaculate square-cut low privet hedge, and white-railed perimeter is crowded with visitors from all over the world. The racing surface is grass, with a sophisticated watering system. The round course measures 2,400 m and the straight course is 1,600 m – the track used for the Grand Criterium, France's top two-year-old race.

But for most international racegoers, and nowadays television racing followers, Longchamp means the Prix de l'Arc de Triomphe, one of the richest races in the world. The 'Arc' is run over a tough 2,400 m for three-year-olds and upwards of either sex and is generally accepted as being the Championship Pattern Race of Europe with the

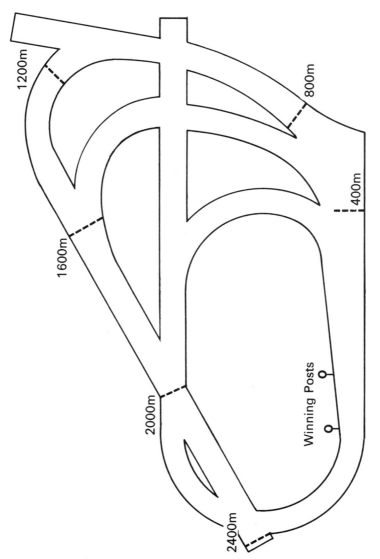

1200m

800m

400m

1600m

2000m

Winning Posts

2400m

Longchamp Racecourse.

winner usually gaining the title of European Horse of the Year. This is a race that calls for a game, quality, well-balanced horse with a good turn of speed which it can sustain up the short homestretch. Most winners have come from a good position on, or just before, the long downhill final turn, and it is rare for a horse to come from behind to take the 'Arc'.

Deauville

The seaside town of Deauville snuggles in a sheltered area of the Channel seaboard on the north-west coast of France, within easy driving distance of the busy port of Le Havre, and of Paris. The town has its own airport nearby at Touques, and with its Casino and beaches is a favourite holiday centre for Parisians. Each year in August, practically the entire Paris racing fraternity emigrates to Deauville for some six weeks of highly competitive racing.

The course, the Hippodrome de la Touques, was created in the nineteenth century by the Duc de Morny, who was responsible for the administration of the first running of the Grand Prix de Paris at Longchamp. Since 1900, the course has been adminstered by the Société d'Encouragement. The Société transfers its offices from Paris to Deauville for the month of August, and, apart from some provincial race-meetings, no other important races are staged elsewhere in France during this period.

The Deauville Yearling Sales are held close to the course in August and, from 1977, were changed to two sessions on the lines of the major British and American Sales. The better bred two-year-olds and yearlings are on offer at the second session.

The most important races staged at Deauville are the Prix Morny and the Grand Prix de Deauville. The Grand Prix, run on the last Sunday of the meeting, is a Group I (Championship) race but the Prix Morny, named after the Duc, is a Group I race for two-year-olds which often gives useful potential form-guides to the following year's European classics.

The course is all grass, flat and oval but with some tight turns. The Norman-style Grandstand and flower-decorated lawns and paddocks give Deauville a charming and delightful holiday atmosphere.

West Germany

In West Germany the sport and thoroughbred breeding is reaching higher levels with each year.The first German Racing Club was formed in 1882 and the German Jockey Club dates back to 1840. But since World War II and the division of Germany, national control has been administered by the Kommissionen des Direktoriums für Vollblutzucht und Rennen und Ihre Aufgaben, which has 16 national committees, with its headquarters in Cologne.

Modern German racing is modelled on the now classic continental system of centralized racing situated round the large cities and popular holiday centres, with State controlled Tote betting providing excellent support for the racecourse facilities, training grounds and the bloodstock industry. Although it would not be true to say the German thoroughbred is yet in the premier European league, German-bred and German-trained horses have had some impressive successes in European Pattern races.

The States and Principalities that became modern Germany were the first countries in Europe to attempt to establish racing and thoroughbred breeding on the lines of the British model. In the early part of the nineteenth century German breeders were importing more stallions from England than the French. The first race meeting organized in Germany was staged at Bad Doberan, Mecklenburg in 1822 but by 1836 regular meetings were being held at Gustrow, Doberan, New Bradenburg, Berlin and Hamburg. Many influential and forceful aristocratic families took up flat-racing and thoroughbred breeding and from the records of that period, it looked very much then as if Germany would become the leader and trend-setter in European racing rather than her neighbour France and, for at least some time, Italy. But the reverse in fact was to happen for, although Germany is a global leader in other horse-sports, she is still some way behind France as a racing power. For Germany, as a horse-racing and breeding nation, has had to cope with three big problems in the last 80 years.

The first of these goes back to the turn of century when it was said, and generally accepted, that a successful bloodstock industry could not exist or thrive without the backing of men of rank and opulence. Germany found such support and as a result Turnus won England's Goodwood Stewards' Cup and Chesterfield Cup in 1850, three years before a French horse won a race in England! The German Derby (Deutsche Derby) was first run at Hamburg in 1869, so a classic programme was well under way. But it seems this early lead was lost because the men of influence were unable to 'follow through'. One of the reasons why this good start went nowhere was the traditional attitudes of the German breeders at the time. They liked, as many modern breeders still do, their thoroughbreds to be big, strong and with plenty of bone, in other words more like a half-bred than a thoroughbred. Their policy was to go for soundness ... and more

128

soundness. A great ideal, but a sound thoroughbred that is not fast enough to win good races is not exactly a commercial proposition.

The second problem is the geographical and geophysical drawbacks of the country itself. Many parts of Germany and what was Prussia, have cold winters and poor sandy soil neither of which is really ideal for the raising of thoroughbreds. The effects of this draw-back can be seen in many of the home-produced two-year-olds which, by English, French and American standards are backward and late-maturing. The third problem to impede the development of the German Thoroughbred-breeding industry was, of course, the effect and aftermath of World War II.

By the end of the 1940's the breeding industry was in a confused state. The 1948 edition of the German *Stud Book*, first compiled in 1847, recorded only 650 thoroughbred mares in West Germany. Hoppegarten, with its first-class training facilities and raceourse and Graditz, the National Stud, were lost behind the Iron Curtain. In 1956 goverment subsidies to racing and breeding and the determination of the German Jockey Club started to pay off. Racecourse attendances increased, as did the Pari-Mutuel turnover, leading to bigger prize money and breeding premiums, which in turn encouraged more investment in bloodstock breeding.

Star Appeal, did a great deal for German racing, although it is perhaps more accurate to describe this very good horse as being internationally bred, for he is by the Italian stallion Appiani II out of a German racemare called Sterna and reared on the lush pastures of Ireland. Star Appeal's brilliant run of victories in 1975 brought him Group I races in Italy, Britain and France, including the Eclipse Stakes and the Prix de l'Arc de Triomphe. The colt raced in the colours of Waldemar Zeitelhack's Stall Moritzberg under trainer Theo Grieper and was ridden by the British jockey Greville Starkey. Star Appeal finished the 1975 European season European and National Horse of the Year, heading the German prize money winners' list with DM 1,320,076 to his credit.

Germany follows the traditional classic three-year-old programme with the Schwarzgold-Rennen (equivalent of the English 1,000 Guineas) run at Dusseldorf in early May, the Henckel-Rennen (equivalent to the English 2,000 Guineas) run at Gelsenkirchen-Horst in late May, the Preis der Diana (equivalent to the English Oaks and the French Prix de Diane) run at Mulheim in early June and the Deutsche Derby run at Hamburg in July.

The biggest problem facing German racing today is not money, or labour but the improvement of the quality and reputation of her home-bred stock. But this is a picture that could change dramatically over the next decade. For prize money in Germany is good, for example, in 1975, the average per horse in training was £1,568, against a British average for the same year of £756. Breeders' premiums are running at 15% of the prize money and training programmes are beginning to show results with more nationals getting into the leading jockey and trainer lists and filling key jobs on stud farms. In years gone by, these important jobs went to mainly imported British labour. Private racehorse ownership is looked upon as flippant in Germany so the majority of the horses run in the colours of a stud farm (Gestüt) or training stables (Stall) but 89% of the brood mares are in small private ownership of four or less mares per owner while over 50% are singly-owned.

Italy

One of the sad stories in European racing has been the rise and fall of Italy as a racing and bloodstock breeding super-power. For some 50 years, thanks to breeders like Federico Tesio, Odoardo Ginistrelli and Count Felice Scheibler and truly great racehorses like Apelle, Nearco and Ribot, the Italian thoroughbred was one of the best in the world.

In 1966 the Dormello-Olgiata Stud, created by the genial Federico Tesio who died in 1954, was so successful that 62.5% of the pedigrees of leading horses in England and Ireland that season had Dormello blood and 36.99% of the pedigrees of Stakes winners in the USA, Canada and Mexico that season contained Dormello blood. An incredible record for any stud in the world but even more so when one considers that the Dormello-Olgiata Stud was in a country where the total brood mare population was only some 800 mares and the annual production of thoroughbred foals running at under 400. It is perhaps for just this reason that such a record could not be sustained forever. For Italy lacks the depth and strength given to any bloodstock industry by the commercial medium sized stud farm such as we see in England, Ireland and France.

The Italian thoroughbred is predominately a middle distance performer and the pattern of Italian racing is framed to test endurance with no 'classic' race being run under 2,000 m, i.e. the Italian Derby at 2,000 m, the Gran Premio d'Italia at 2,000 m and the Italian St Leger over 2,400 m and the best three-year-olds often competing in other major races against their elders over distances of nearly 3,200 m.

But Italy is a very old 'racing' country, eastern horses were used long before the idea of creating the thoroughbred was thought of and organized racing has been practised in Florence and Naples since 1837 although Milan is now the main racing and breeding centre. A rennaissance of the Italian racehorse may not be all that far away for prize money and premuims have increased considerably in recent years and Italian bloodstock buyers have been very active in the past two years at the Dublin, Deauville and Newmarket Sales.

6
Racing in Australasia

The bloodstock industries of Australia and New Zealand are so closely interwoven and geared to each other's needs that whatever happens to one directly relates to the other. New Zealand tends to play the role of producer and her big brother, Australia, the practioner with the performance test-bed.

Australia's first official race meeting was held at Hyde Park, Sydney in October 1810 and the first recorded race meetings in New Zealand were staged by the first British settlers on the beach in Wellington Harbour in January 1840. Racing in New Zealand became seriously organized in the 1890's when the metropolitan clubs and provincial clubs were affiliated to the Racing Conference. This conference formulated the style and pattern of New Zealand racing that exists today.

Racing in Australia, although it was put together by one of the first English Turf-barons Admiral Rous, is nearer to the American-style in application than it is to the now rather old-fashioned parent model practised in Britain. The similarities are in the courses (most of them flat and oval, many have 'dirt' racing surfaces) the emphasis on time-training, the powerful and rich centralized State Racing Boards and the track training facilities, as against groups of private stable yards clustered around a natural training area such as downs or heaths. The Australians like good, fast racehorses, but tough ones, and over the years the Australasian Thoroughbred has gained a world-wide reputation for honesty and toughness.

But there is a much more important difference which complicates any comparison of the Australian/New Zealand racehorse with his European and North American cousin, and that is the fact that one lives in the Northern Hemisphere and the other in the Southern Hemisphere. This fact, in the breeding industry, makes them two worlds apart. The covering season for brood mares falls in the spring and early summer of each year. The foals born in the spring are Early Foals and those born in the summer are Late Foals but all thoroughbreds in the Northern Hemisphere become yearlings on January 1 following their birth and from then on all share the same birthday of New Year's Day. But these seasons fall on an entirely different cycle in the Southern Hemisphere, so although covering the mares takes place in their spring and early summer cycle it is, in fact, the fall and winter in the Northern Hemisphere and the Australasian thoroughbred foal does not become a yearling until August 1 following his birth, and from then on all Southern Hemisphere thoroughbreds share the same birthday of August 1.

There have been examples since 1880's of Australian breeders having their mares covered to Northern Hemisphere time and the products of those matings sent to race in America and Europe with considerable success. The older the horses get, of course, the less marginal is the 'age' difference. In modern times, the 1970s, many leading European and American breeders with stud farm interests in Australia have stood their stallions in Europe or the States to Northern Hemisphere time and then shipped them to Australia to stand at Southern Hemisphere time, thereby getting two covering seasons out of them. So far, those who who have tried this system have found that there are no ill- or side-effects on the stallions.

The Australian racegoer is a devout gambler and takes his racing very seriously. Not for him the roulette-style numbers betting; he studies form, track-times, weights and the betting-odds. For the Australian racegoer is one of the few in the international race-game that has the best of both worlds. On the racecourse he can bet with the Tote at computer-rated odds, knowing that his losses are going to a good cause – State taxes, prize money, breeders' premiums, racetrack and training improvements – and off the racecourse he can take on the more traditional bookmakers in the betting-parlours of the cities and large towns. The two systems, private enterprise and State control, seem to work side by side in Australia very well.

Some idea of the popularity of racing in Australia is given by the 82,000 paying customers that flock to Flemington racecourse, Melbourne, Victoria, on Melbourne Cup day each year, and the enormous crowds that can be seen each weekend at the superb Randwick racecourse in Sydney, New South Wales.

The Sydney Turf Club which organized the first official race-meeting at Hyde Park, Sydney, way back in 1810 is the oldest Turf Club on the continent. But much of its power was soon taken over by the Australian Racing and Jockey Club which was formed by Governor Sir Ralph Darling, and in 1840 the Australian Race Committee was formed to administer the sport. Since then though as a national governing body, rather in the same way as the American Jockey Club, it has been somewhat weakened by the comparative strength of the State Racing Boards.

There are no set classics in Australia in the same way as Europe and America. For example, in Britain, the 1,000 Guineas, 2,000 Guineas, Oaks, Derby and St Leger make up the national programme of classic races for three-year-old colts and fillies. In Australia each State Racing Board has its own classic programme, e.g. Victoria has its own Derby at Flemington, and so on. This individual classic programme is a direct result of the continent being divided into states in the 1860's. But 'Cup' races, like the Caulfield (2,400 m) and the distance handicaps like the Melbourne and Sydney Cups both run over 3,200 m, tend to carry more prestige in Australia than the more traditional classic racing performance tests. For generations Australian breeders have adhered consistently to the original policy of the Australian Race Committee to breed horses of strength and endurance. For around 1840 when the Australian Race Committee was formed it issued a manifesto stating the policy that it hoped to encourage the Australian breeding industry to follow:

'The nature of this country is eminently adapted to meet the purposes of the horse breeder, and there can be little doubt in the minds of those who have considered the subject with attention that as soon as the number of horses bred here shall be sufficiently extensive to supply our colonial demand, we shall find in the neighbouring settlements and in India a sure and steady market for all our surplus; but to give our horses a reputation in foreign countries we must show to the world of what efforts they are capable, and prove that we can devote both judgement and attention to the improvement of the breed.'

The committee declared its intention to encourage breeders to produce the type of horse that combined strength, endurance, and the maximum speed. This, in a sentence, accurately describes the qualities of the Australian and New Zealand racehorse of today. A horse that has proved he has all three of these qualities in racing, trotting, pacing and steeplechasing.

The racing business in Australia is now a billion dollar industry but all breeding stock is in private hands, there is no government-owned or controlled national stud except for two small state-owned Arabian studs at Hawksbury and Gatton Agricultural Colleges. Most of the leading farms are situated in areas where the annual rainfall is sufficient to support good pasture, like New South Wales and Victoria. Although many of the modern stud farms now practise intensive grass management and have very sophisticated water con-

Mares and foals at Kentucky Stud, near Grafton, NSW.

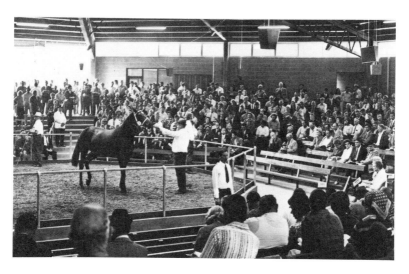

Annual yearling sales at Melbourne.

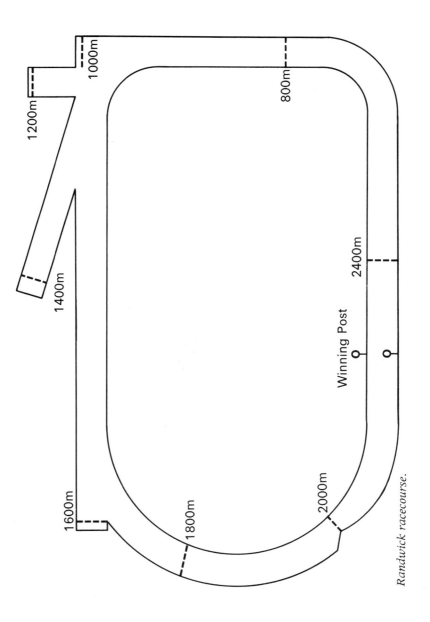

Randwick racecourse.

servation systems. Annual yearling sales are held in the capital cities which usually include quite a number of unregistered clean-bred stock. Horses other than registered thoroughbreds can be raced providing they are recorded with the Australian Jockey Club but their progeny are not accepted for entry in the *Australian Stud Book*. The largest yearling sales are held in Sydney, New South Wales, where some 1,500 yearlings are sold annually and the average price paid per head is around $A6,000 to $A8,000. Melbourne, Brisbane, Adelaide and Perth are not all that far behind with some 600 to 1,000 yearlings offered each year. American buyers are always in attendance at these sales and several Australian horses have become famous stud names in the USA.

The Australian Bloodhorse Breeders' Association published some interesting figures in 1974 showing that of the 427 yearlings offered that year at Adelaide, the dams of 215 were winners on the racecourse before retiring to stud, 85 were from unraced broodmares and a further 85 were bred from New Zealand broodmares and 109 lots were first foals of their dams, while a further 77 were second progeny. These throw quite interesting light on the Australian breeders emphasis on racetrack performance in their blood lines and the continuing influence of New Zealand Thoroughbreds.

Both the North and South Islands of New Zealand are ideal for the production of thoroughbreds but over recent years New Zealand breeders, and trainers, have favoured the richer more populated North Island for their activities. Here the climate is temperate, promoting good grass growth throughout the year, with high mineral content land essential for the growth of good bone in young animals thus making New Zealand a first-class breeding ground for thoroughbred horses.

At the annual yearling sales in 1979 from 350 lots sold, 200 went to Australia and well over 50 to other countries. From those which stay in the country New Zealand trainers still manage to win their fair share of Australian stakes races, including several Melbourne Cups. The quality of New Zealand racehorses was well advertized in Europe in 1977 when the very useful middle distance performer Balmerino made a successful tour of Italy, Britain, France and America which included running second in the Prix de l'Arc de Triomphe.

There are some 700 racecourses in Australia but many of these are no more than 'bush' tracks with very few facilities for racing of any high standard. It is on the 'bush' circuit, however, that many of the very talented Australian jockeys learn their craft. But the major courses such as Randwick and Flemington are as, and in some cases

Randwick racecourse from the grandstand.

more, luxurious than their counterpart in Europe and America. During the racing season the horses are moved from one centre to the other. For example, as racing finishes on the Adelaide circuit the training strings will set off for Sydney or Brisbane. The horses are trained mainly on the track in the mornings similar to the American system.

The Melbourne Cup is, perhaps, Australasia's most famous and coveted race. The 'Cup' is a handicap run over 3,200 m on Felmington racecourse, Victoria and was first staged in 1861. New Zealand's major race is the Auckland Cup run at the end of December at Wellington. The Wellington Club stages five meetings in January, March, May, July and October and runs its own classics, Derby and Oaks etc.

Exercise swimming pool for horses at Caulfield racecourse, Melbourne.

7
Racing in Japan

Japan imported Australian and American thoroughbreds as far back as 1907 but it was not until the post World War II years that the nation became of any importance within the international racing game. The stallions Shian-Mar, Tournasol, Primero and Theft were imported between the years 1920 and 1938 and it was these that became the tap-root bloodline of the Japanese Thoroughbred. But the Japanese are more the buyers of top-class bloodstock than producers of truly international standard racehorses. Yet it must be said that if Japanese breeders apply the same thoroughness and commercial intelligence to their breeding policies as Japanese businessmen have done in other areas it would be no surprise to see them emerge in years to come as premier bloodstock producers.

After World War II there were only some 52 stallions and 550 broodmares, with an annual foal production of under 300, in the country. But Japan was determined to build a thriving, financially strong, thoroughbred breeding and sporting industry. During the 1960's owners, breeders, the Japan Racing Association and the Ministry of Agriculture, went on a buying spree at the racing world's best sales: Newmarket, Ballsbridge, Deauville, Keeneland, Saratoga and Sydney. And at the top of their shopping lists was quality and proven racetrack performance. The strength of the Yen created what must be one of the commercial 'miracles' of the twentieth century sporting world.

As the Swinging Sixties came to a close, foal production was up to nearly 4,000 and western classic horses like Hard Ridden, Larkspur, Nimbus, Galcador, Pearl Diver, Parthia, Lavandin (all winners of the Epsom Derby), Philius II, Tamanar, Rapace (winners of the French Derby), Hindostan, Panaslipper, Chamier, Fidalgo (winners of the Irish Derby) and Iron Liege (winner of the Kentucky Derby) were standing at Japanese Studs and producing good, winning stock. Two factors, in particular, have influenced this unrivalled expansion, the Japanese public's tremendous enthusiasm for betting and racing and the outstanding post-war success of Japan as a major industrial nation.

The weighing room at a Japanese racecourse.

The Japan Racing Association shrewdly took advantage of these facts by using its rake-off from the Pari-Mutuel to increase prize money, provide incentive schemes and improve racecourses and training facilities. Through a consolation-prize system no horse starts a race without earning something! The average prize money per horse in training is running at around £2,000, higher than that of the USA and France.

In Japan, horse-racing and all its allied services and products such as bloodstock breeding, is adminstered by the Japan Racing Association. The association is a non-profit making organization supervised by the Ministry of Agriculture and Forestry. The Minister appoints all officials and representatives and the JRA operates twelve national racecourses plus the training centres at Ritto in Western Japan and at Tokyo. In addition there are also some 42 'country' racecourses and these are run by town councils. About a quarter of the Pari-Mutuel (first legalized in 1923) turnover is invested back into the sport through the official bodies and a contribution to training expenses is paid direct to the trainer of each runner.

Most of the stud farms are in the Hidaka and Iburi districts on the

North Island of Hokkaido, the traditional breeding areas of native horses. The climate is not the best for rearing thoroughbred stock and the cost of production is high, as mares, foals and yearlings have to be housed most of the time. But Hokkaido-bred horses seem to be well-grown as two-year-olds and often train on well up to their four-year-old season.

Every racing system seems to be able to produce its own 'world-beater' that has that special magic which captures the hearts of even the most hardened racegoer. Leading stakes winner Takeshiba-O, known to race-fans as 'The Monster', won practically everything worth winning in Japan in the late 60's but Japan's real wonder-horse was the handsome Speed Symboli. This colt travelled to Laurel Park, USA, in 1967 and finished a creditable fifth in the Washington International Invitation race behind the good American horse Fort Marcy. In 1969 Speed Symboli travelled to England to run in the King George VI and Queen Elizabeth Stakes at Ascot and again finished fifth, this time behind the classy Park Top.

The pattern of Japanese racing is woven around a programme of classic races for 3-year-olds similar to the European model. The equivalent of the 2,000 Guineas is run over 2,000 m at Nakayama, the 1,000 Guineas equivalent over 1,600 m on Hanshin racecourse in the Kansai region of Western Japan and the Derby and Oaks equivalents over 2,400 m at Tokyo racecourse. The Derby was first run in 1933 and is now worth some £95,000 to the winning owner.

The sub-tropical climate of the islands controls the timing of the racing season. In the rainy season in mid-June racing is not possible and in the high, humid summer temperatures the sport almost comes to a halt. There are some race-meetings staged at 'country' courses and on the island of Hokkaido during these times but the main season operates in two periods. The first, the spring season, comes to a close with the running of the Japanese Derby at the end of May and the second, the autumn season, opens in September and closes in December. In the 1960's two custom-built and designed centres for the care and training of thoroughbreds were created. The first, Ritto Training Centre was opened in 1969 and the second near Tokyo was completed in the early 70's. The Ritto Training Centre, sited near Lake Biwa in Western Japan, is a self-contained unit on a 410-acre site with apartments, a supermarket, school, hospital, and stabling for some 2,000 racehorses. The staff of trainers, sub-trainers, jockeys, work-riders, handlers, apprentices, veterinarians, assistant veterinarians and farriers, and their families make Ritto a completely racing-orientated town with a population of nearly 5,000 people.

A great deal of intelligent thought was given to the creation of Japan's *Cité du Cheval*, allowing for the very hot Japanese summers. So the loose-boxes in which the thoroughbreds are housed are set out in sanded rows with two doors for each box to help good air-flow in the summer. Each independent unit comprises 20 loose-boxes, a tack room, forage store and a house for a jockey or trainer and his family. There are five training tracks, four with a dirt surface and distances of 1,450 m, 1,600 m, 1,800 m, and 2,200 m and a turf gallop of 1,950 m. A grandstand has been built where trainers can view their horses when working on the gallops, with facilities for the racing press – an idea European racing would do itself no harm to copy. All the horses, when in training, wear coloured saddle-cloths indicating their ages and identification number, which must make the racing journalist's job a great deal easier. Training sessions start, as in the South of France, at four o'clock in the morning and on race-days some strings get the first lot out even earlier! During the hot summers the training gallops are flood-lit so that work-outs can be done in the cool of the late evening air.

An intensive racing programme and concentrated centres of training and breeding mean that the many contagious viruses that thoroughbreds can suffer from or carry can spread more easily and affect racing and breeding programmes more dramatically than say less nationally centralized systems such as the Australian State-by-State organization. If, for example, there was an outbreak of equine influenza in New South Wales it could be contained in that region by stopping horses from that area travelling to race-meetings in another state and by putting a temporary ban on horses and personnel from entering the infected area. The Japan Racing Association and Ministry of Agriculture and Forestry has taken steps against this hazard by building one of the finest equine clinics in the world at Ritto. The clinic can handle 150 horses per day, plus those in quarentine. All new horses arriving at Ritto must go through the clinic before entering training, and all racehorses in Japan must have a current health certificate from the Equine Clinic.

The Ritto Clinic is also one of the most advanced in the world on the treatment of fractures. The centre's veterinary surgeons have developed a bone-pinning technique whereby the fractured fragments are 'transplanted' back to the main bone using pins and bolts. Many of their successful operations in this field have allowed a seriously injured racehorse to continue his career, or at the very least, kept him or her fit enough to be used for breeding successfully. Ritto is continually researching this field and, thanks to its veterinarians,

Racehorse arriving at night at the Ritto Training Centre near Tokyo.

the day may not be far off when certain limb or other bone fractures will not mean the immediate destruction of the horse. The Japanese equine scientists are also carrying out some very effective work on the physical therapy of respiratory, heart and muscle disorders using ultra-short wave, ultrasonic and acupuncture treatments.

8
Racing in Other Countries

South America
Although the first horses were brought to the South American continent by the Spanish in the fifteenth and sixteenth centuries, this vast country of 13 independent States with its mountains, jungles and pampas grasslands has become over the centuries as much the land of the horse and gaucho as Texas has become the spirit of the ever sun-setting American West.

In Argentina, for example, there are now over four million horses of various breeds, with the majority being Criollos, descendants of the original Spanish stock. According to United Nations figures there are nine million horses in Brazil, the fifth largest state in the world.

The Latin Americans love their racing, and the breeding of thoroughbreds, once the fun-hobby of the very wealthy, is a major industry run on the most up-to-date principles. This is especially so of the Argentine. There are 40 major racecourses with two superb tracks in the city of Buenos Aires. The Argentinian thoroughbred sales are now attended by top buyers from all over South and Central America, the USA and Canada and the bloodstock business in Venezuela, Brazil and Argentina is very much an export-to-survive industry. Taking the Argentine again as our example, this mineral-rich country with a human population density of some 26 persons per square mile has taken full advantage of its immense pastoral regions in the temperate zone of South America to produce world-class thoroughbreds and become one of the world's biggest producers with a rate of nearly 6,000 foals per year.

Although the tap-root stock has to be imported, mainly from Britain and France, South American breeders have made rapid progress from 224 mares and under 300 stallions in 1893 when the *Argentine Stud Book* (*SBA-Stud Book Argentino*) was first published, to a total number of thoroughbreds of some 70,000 and registered TB foals running at over 7,500 by the mid-1970's. One of the most famous and successful to be bred in Argentina, and he is by no means the only one, was the mighty Forli. Forli won the Argentine Quadruple Crown, the Polla de Potrillos (equivalent to the British

2,000 Guineas), the Gran Premio Jockey Club, the Gran Premio Nacional (Derby) and the Gran Premio Carlos Pellegrini in 1966. He was then exported to the USA for nearly a million dollars. Forli, a colt that traced back to the potent Hyperion on his sire's side, raced successfully as a four-year-old in the Northern Hemisphere, although by Southern Hemisphere reckoning he was in fact still a 3-year-old. He was then retired to stand at the Claiborne Stud Farm in Kentucky. Forli's son Forego was Horse of the Year in the USA three years running, and at the close of the 1976 season he had scored 29 wins and 14 placings from 48 outings, earning his Lazy S Ranch owners more than $1,655,000. In recent years Argentine and Venezuela-bred racehorses have had tremendous success in American stakes races.

South Africa
Lord Charles Somerset, Governor of South Africa, was the key figure in regularizing thoroughbred racing in South Africa in the early years of the nineteenth century, although there had been racing of a sort in the colony before the end of the eighteenth century.

South African racing follows the traditional pattern of three-year-olds classic races. The South African Derby was first run in 1885 over nine furlongs but is now staged in December over the full 'Derby' distance of $1\frac{1}{2}$ m, but there are more two-year-old races, sprints, handicaps and weight-for-age races than middle distance or long distance races in the South African calendar.

For various reasons beyond the control of the sport, South African horses are not seen a great deal on the American or European circuits but Hawaii, bred at the Platberg Stud, Colesberg in the Eastern Province and sired by the Italian imported stallion Utrillo, spent some time in training in the United States. Hawaii finished second in the 1969 Washington International Invitation championship race at Laurel Park and won the important Man O'War Stakes.

Hong Kong
Hong Kong, along with Japan, is one of the real success stories of modern racing. Racing in the tiny but densely populated and highly commercially successful colony goes back over 120 years and the Royal Hong Kong Jockey Club, with its lovely address of Sports Road, Happy Valley, is over 80 years old. Racing in Hong Kong is not so much geared to the world's bloodstock markets as to the protectorate's social services. Here the racehorse and the gambler help the ambitious, the infirm, the young and the neglected.

The computerized on-course tote betting system, the most advanced

The Parade Ring at Sha Tin Racecourse, Hong Kong.

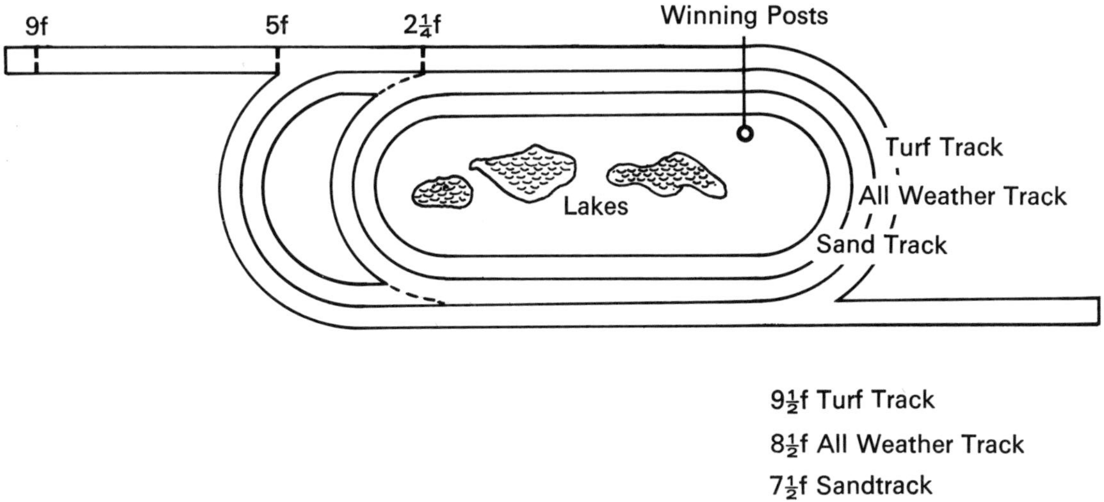

Turf Track

All Weather Track

Sand Track

Winning Posts

Lakes

$2\frac{1}{4}$f

5f

9f

$9\frac{1}{2}$f Turf Track

$8\frac{1}{2}$f All Weather Track

$7\frac{1}{2}$f Sandtrack

Sha Tin Racecourse, Hong Kong.

in the world, plus off-course betting, both the responsibility of the Jockey Club, earned the public purse $301.3 million through betting duty in 1977. The surplus the Jockey Club is able to produce from the efficient management of its racing and betting services has also increased and become available for the development of recreational facilities and many other community projects. The biggest of these community projects, Ocean Park, attracted nearly two million visitors in its opening year. During 1977 subventions to some 74 charities were increased by the largest overall percentage ever.

Apart from the Jubilee Sports Centre, the RHJC's initiative is also evident in a number of exciting projects which are outside the range of normal Government activities and beyond the means of private organizations.

At Pokfulam, for example, the club has announced plans for the construction of a centre which will be the headquarters for a variety of organizations concerned with the physically handicapped. On land provided by the Government the RHJC will build accommodation, swimming and sporting facilities, as well as a riding school for both the public and handicapped persons. The club has committed $7.5 million to this project. As a demonstration of the scope of its interests another $10 million has been given to a trust fund which will be used to encourage the development of musical talent in Hong Kong.

The club, then, plays four important roles: administering and controlling racing as a sport to the highest possible standards; playing its part in social policy by diverting money from illegal gambling operations; as a revenue earner for Government; and making surplus funds from betting available to good community causes in an efficient and imaginative way.

The pride of the Royal Hong Kong Jockey Club is the new Sha Tin racecourse and training centre opened in 1978. The construction of the Sha Tin racecourse was a massive undertaking. The operation was not simple. Behind the 6,000 ft long seawall 16 million tons of earth and rock were dumped by a fleet of lorries which at the peak of the reclamation programme were tipping a load into the sea every eight seconds. Some 1 million tons of trapped marine mud had to be removed during the process.

The end result was a racecourse of the highest standards with up-to-date spectator facilities of every kind, including a well-planned road and rail system. The infield of the track has been landscaped with lakes, flower-beds and trees.

There is a 1,000 m straight giving Hong Kong's 30,000-odd racegoers a brand new experience of speed plus an eight-storey grandstand, an all-weather track, sanded training gallops and ten two-storey stable blocks each accommodating 50 horses.

But racing still continues at Happy Valley, which dates back to the first half of the nineteenth century, and maintains its special charm with the high-rise blocks towering over it, the Rock, and the droll procession of horses down from the stables and across the tram lines.

9
The Jockeys

The riding technique of the early jockeys was a blend of classical equitation and the more natural balanced seat of the hunting field. These serious looking lean-faced men sat tall and straight in their saddles, carrying a long whalebone whip and spurs with their narrow legs hanging down to their natural length.

One of the great masters of the style was Samuel Chifney Jnr (1753–1807). Sam was born in Norfolk and entered Fox's yard at Newmarket as an apprentice. He won the Derby on Skyscraper in 1789 and in 1773 he wrote of himself, 'I can ride horses in a better manner in a race to beat others than any person ever known in my time'. Chifney was one of the first race-riders to exploit the method of riding a 'waiting race'.

But the first real superstar of the silks was the legendary Fred Archer (1857–1886), champion jockey of England for 13 seasons. 'The Tinman', as he was known to racegoers, was almost illiterate but he was an outstanding horseman. During his career he won 2,748 races, including six St Legers, five Derbys, four 2,000 Guineas and two 1,000 Guineas but he was continually troubled by weight problems. At only 29-years-old the gifted Archer took his own life on Newmarket Heath while in a depressed state brought on by his obsessive dedication to beat the weighing room scales.

The modern jockey, throughout the world, rides on a lighter forward-cut saddle designed for riding with short leathers. The short stirrup-leathers make the jockey's job of balancing and controlling a racehorse easier while crouching low to cut down wind resistance.

James Todhunter Sloan (1874–1933), an American jockey, is credited with the invention of the modern racing seat. Tod Sloan brought his crouching style of race-riding to Great Britain in 1897. It was very successful and Tod soon had an army of imitators. Sloan, like the twentieth century American jockey, was a great judge of pace and a master of the difficult technique of 'waiting' in front of his field.

The American jockey, and many Australians, crouch much lower to their horses than their European colleagues. This more streamlined style is encouraged by their fast oval and level tracks.

Fred Archer.

Tod Sloan.

Many great names are recorded in the sporting history books, names like Steve Donoghue, Tommy Weston, Manny Mercer, Michael Beary, Freddy Lane, the Smith brothers Eph and Doug, Charlie Elliott, Charlie Smirke, Freddy Palmer, Brownie Carslake, Marcel Garcia, Harry Wragg, Bobby Martin, and many others. But some names are just that bit bigger than others and two in particular reigned supreme in their riding days.

One of the American turf's all-time greats was the Yorkshire-born Johnny Longden, rider of some 5,000 winners. Britain's daddy-of-them-all was Gordon Richards, born in Shropshire in 1904. Gordon Richards was designed to be a jockey, he stood no more than 4 ft 11 in in his racing boots but he had the strength of a man much taller and heavier. Sir Gordon, knighted in 1953 – the first professional jockey to be so honoured, was British Champion jockey 26 times in 34 years of race-riding and won 4,870 races from 21,834 rides including three 2,000 gns and 1,000 gns, two Oaks, five St Legers and one Epsom Derby. But Sir Gordon's career was full of records, in 1947 he rode 269 winners breaking Fred Archer's record of 246 winners during the 1885 season and in 1933, twelve years after riding his first winner, he scored the longest winning streak of 12, riding the last race winner at Nottingham on October 3, six winners out of six races on October 4 at Chepstow and the first five races at Chepstow the following day. Sir Gordon, now retired but still very involved in the game as a racing and bloodstock adviser, rode for some of Britain's greatest trainers like Fred Darling (1884–1953) producer of 19 classic winners including seven Epsom Derby winners and Sir Noel Murless (born 1916) who equalled Fred Darling's record of 19 classic winners and headed the British trainers' list nine times between 1948 and 1973. In a brilliant 41-year career Sir Noel won over £3 million in prize money for his patrons.

In 1949 a dapper little 19-year-old Texan rode his first winner, Shafter V, at San Francisco's Golden Gate Fields racetrack. His name was William Lee 'The Shoe' Shoemaker and if ever a sportsman earned the title 'legend in his own lifetime' it is the 4 ft $11\frac{1}{2}$ in, 98 lb, Shoemaker. 'The Shoe' is the only jockey in the world to ride more than 7,500 winners and the list is still growing; so far he has won over $70 million for his owners. Willie is as popular in Europe as he is in the States, his quiet, natural style and deadly accurate judgement of pace is a match-winner no matter what system of racing he finds himself in. Willie was raised in Texas and entered trainer George Reeves' yard at the age of 14 and he attributes much of his success to the fact that he was given an old-fashioned apprenticeship,

Sir Gordon Richards.

Sir Noel Murless, trainer of many classic winners.

learning all the duties of a stable lad as well as the art of jockeyship.

Today there is a young group of American jockeys coming up that do not give much away to the 'Shoemakers' when it comes to ability. Many of them are Latin Americans but one home-grown youngster really going places is Steve Cauthen. Kentucky-raised Cauthen has, like Shoemaker and Longden, proved that the American jockey's horsemanship and clock-conscious mind is as effective on the European tracks as it is on the sunshine circuits of Florida and California.

While still at school in Kentucky the then 16-year-old Steve Cauthen won 240 races on the flat within a period of six months in 1977, earning himself some $150,000 in bonuses and collecting for his racehorse owners nearly one and a half million dollars. The polite, quietly spoken Cauthen went on to even bigger things the following season when he was associated with the great American classic horse Affirmed, the most valuable thoroughbred in the world when syndicated for $14.4 million in November 1978. For the 1979 season he signed a lucrative contract with owner Robert Sangster to ride for him in Europe. Steve was based with Newmarket trainer Barry Hills and, although he did not have quite the sparkling season forcast for him through the Hills' stable being dogged by virus problems, the 5 ft tall, 95 lb Jockey won a classic and impressed European racegoers.

In post Second World War years, the Australian jockey has become one of the most sought after on the international circuit. This 'young' nation produces jockeys capable of adapting quickly to the European or American systems. They are natural horseman with superb hands and they can ride a waiting race or go off in front. Like their American colleagues they are masters at judging pace to the stopwatch. Many top Australians have ridden with great success in Europe, men like Edgar Britt, rider of six classic winners in England during the 1940's and 50's and W. 'Rae' Johnstone, who was based in France, and a big race specialist, winning 10 English classics including the Epsom Derby three times between 1948 and 1956. Arthur 'Scobie' Breasley became English champion and won the Epsom Derby on Santa Claus in 1964 and Charlottown in 1966. George Moore rode for Noel Murless in 1967 and in that one season won the 2,000 Guineas on Royal Palace, the 1,000 Guineas on Fleet and the Epsom Derby on Royal Palace, plus nearly all the leading English handicaps. Ron Hutchinson spent several years in Europe riding with great success as first jockey to England's then senior Jockey Club member, the late Duke of Norfolk.

France, too, has produced more than her fair-share of riders up to international standards like Jacques Doyasbere, Paul Blanc, Marcel Garcia, Roger Poincelet, Georges Bridgeland and Freddie Palmer. But the life of the French jockey is very different from that of the English rider. There is very little travelling involved in his daily routine and as most of the training yards are 'one-owner' enterprises, the jockeys tend to be contract riders as against free-lances booked per ride. There are race-meetings throughout the Paris season practically every day including Sundays but little evening racing. It is very rare for a French jockey to ride at two race-meetings in one day whereas for the English jockey this is quite a normal part of his working life. In the provinces race meetings are usually staged at weekends and on holidays, with some mid-week racing, but it is not often that a leading Parisian jockey will ride in the provinces unless booked to ride in a valuable Grand Prix like the Grand Prix de Marseilles or Lyons.

From the point of view of money, the French jockey in general is better off and more secure in his professional life than, say, the English or Irish jockey. Besides his retainer and riding fees, he gets a percentage of *all* prize money won, including place, which is very high in France and these funds are stopped at source for him by the Société d'Encouragement. As a licensed rider he is registered with the Ministry of Agriculture and therefore qualifies for full social security benefits.

French racing is fortunate in having several top-class race-riders with two, Yves St Martin and Freddie Head, of really world-class standard. Yves St Martin started his apprenticeship with Chantilly trainer François Mathet in 1955 and rode his first winner at Le Tremblay on July 26, 1958 when he was only 18-years-old. This consistent and intelligent rider has headed the French jockeys' list many times including an uninterrupted run from 1962 to 1969. Yves, born at Agen in the South of France in 1941, became an international star in 1962 when he won the Washington Laurel Park International in America aboard Match III, and the British Oaks on M. Goulandris's Manade, trained by Jean Lieux. The following year he won the Epsom Derby on M. Dupre's Relko, trained by his old 'master' François Mathet. Yves, the 'pin-up boy' of European racing, has ridden the winners of nearly all of Europe's major championship races such as the Prix de l'Arc de Triomphe and the King George VI and Queen Elizabeth Stakes. French and English classics have been associated with some of the greatest horses of international racing such as Allez France and Pawnese, the flying filly.

Freddie Head, like Britain's Lester Piggott, was almost bred to be a jockey. He served his apprenticeship with his father Alec Head and

S. Cauthen on Tap on Wood winning the 2,000 Guineas at Newmarket.

G. Starkey, on Homeward Bound, entering the Epsom winner's enclosure after the Oaks.

rode his first winner at Fontainebleau, April 13, 1964. His grandfather was a leading trainer, his uncle a top jockey and trainer, and his sister is also a successful trainer. So it is no wonder that this forceful and determined rider has been French champion several times and has booted home the winners of classic races, championship races and, so far, three winners of the rich Prix de l'Arc de Triomphe.

Great Britain and Ireland have always been the traditional producers of good jockeys and wherever there is organized racing it is almost odds-on, to crib a betting term, that at least one of the top riders will be an Englishman or an Irishman. The modern stars are articulate, bright young men like Willie Carson, Pat Eddery, and Paul Cook, and shrewd senior men like Greville Starkey and the 1979 champion 45-year-old Joe Mercer. But the superstar of British racing, and the international circuit, is the jet-setting Lester Piggott.

Lester Piggott, champion jockey nine times, served his apprenticeship with his father Keith and rode his first winner at 13 years of age. Only five years later the 'boy wonder' of the English racecourses won his first Epsom Derby on the American-bred Never Say Die. Over a long and glorious career the tall, rather shy, Lester, born on November 5, 1935, has won over 20 English classic races including eight Epsom Derbys, a record for the great race, and has ridden on practically every major racetrack in the world. But the genial Lester, who was given an OBE in Queen Elizabeth II's honours list for his services to the sport, has ridden some of the finest thoroughbreds ever bred: the Vincent O'Brien trained Nijinsky, British Triple Crown winner in 1970; the Noel Murless trained Crepello, winner of the 1957 2,000 Guineas and Derby; Sir Ivor, another Vincent O'Brien product, winner of the 1968 2,000 Guineas, Derby and Washington Laurel Park International race; and many many others that would fill a book on their own.

For most racing experts Lester Piggott is the greatest jockey of all time with the temperament for the big occasion, and uncanny ability to 'read' a race accurately, outstanding judgement of pace and brilliant timing.

10
Betting

Basically there are two main systems of betting in the racing world, by Totalisator or 'Pool' betting, and by Bookmakers. The first bookmaker to operate on a racecourse it seems was a man named Ogden who set up 'shop' on Newmarket racecourse, England in 1795. The family business of Tattersalls, now bloodstock agents and auctioneers, was created by Richard Tattersall in 1766 and, apart from holding sales in London for racehorses, hunters and driving horses, their emporium became a social meeting place of racing men and wagers were often struck on the races of the day. Tattersalls eventually gave their name to the main betting ring on the fashionable English racecourses now known as Tattersalls enclosure. The firm of Tattersalls drew up the first regulations and rules on betting transactions in 1886 and to this day the 'Tattersalls Committee' has been the absolute body on all matters and arguments involving betting. The Committee is supported by the Jockey Club and its membership is made up of bookmakers, members of the Jockey Club and the reporters responsible for returning the starting prices from the racecourse.

Bookmakers in Britain since the late 1960's are required by law to pay a betting tax to the Treasury which in turn they deduct from all winning bets. They are also required to pay a tax on turnover to the Horserace Betting Levy Board and these monies are ploughed back into the sport.

But the most important area of betting in Britain is in the off-course wagers that are placed at the 12,000-odd betting shops that can be seen in practically every major town and city in the country. This style of betting dates back to the first half of the nineteenth century when street bookmakers and wagering on private premises or gentlemen's clubs was, in fact, illegal. It was not until 1961 when the Betting and Gaming Act was introduced that off-course betting became legal.

Some countries operate a tote monopoly, others a sort of half-way house with bookmakers allowed on the course and the tote monopolizing the off-course betting or vice versa. Australia, Belgium, India and South Africa use this happy mixture system whereas in Great

Crowd in the betting ring between events at an Australian country race meeting at Westernport Bay.

Britain and Ireland, the original homelands of horse-racing, the tote and bookmakers have to compete against each other both on the course and off it. The British tote was set up by an Act of Parliament in 1928 to provide an alternative betting service to the bookmakers. The Totalisator is a semi-government body responsible to the Home Secretary and through his office to Parliament. The Home Office appoints the members of the Tote Board. The tote first appeared on English racecourses at Newmarket and Carlisle in 1929 but in 1972 by act of Parliament, the Totalisator and Horse Race Betting Levy Board was established giving the tote a greater freedom in the services it could offer its customers, and to control the channelling of monies back into the sport. The tote in Britain is becoming more popular with racing fans each season and the total turnover per annum is well in excess of £50 million.

In France all betting comes under the state controlled Pari-mutuel and as other forms of bookmaking were made illegal in 1891, the French racing and bloodstock industry now benefits from its own efficient pool which provides the financial resources it needs. The most popular bet in France is the weekly *Tiercé*. One race is selected each week for the *tiercé* and the French sporting and daily press give an enormous amount of space to this race, giving form-ratings on all

163

the runners in great detail and competing very hard to tip the *tiercé*. The object of the bet is to forcast the first three in the race either in correct order, or out of order. The big pay-out is to the tickets naming the first three in order but one fifth of the pool makes up the consolation winnings for those tickets naming the first three in any order. The *tiercé* is calculated on the unit of 1 franc. In 1976 the Prix de l'Arc de Triomphe was a *tiercé* race and on that day alone some 97 million francs was gambled on the race.

In the USA the Pari-mutuel betting system is used and controlled by the State Betting Boards. The standard bets are a 'win', or 'place' (first or second) and a 'show' (first, second or third) but many racetracks have introduced what are called 'exotic' bets to attract bigger crowds at the track. These are the Exacta, often called the Perfects (a straight forecast bet naming the first two in the correct order of finishing) in nominated races and the Trifecta, where the bettor must select the first three in a race in the correct order, a simpler version of the French *tiercé* bet.

Tote monopoly off-course and bookmakers, in special enclosures, on-course, is the system used in Australia. The off-course betting parlours send back their totals some 20 minutes before a race starts and these figures are included on the large Totalisator Boards on the racecourse showing the dividend for each runner at any precise moment. But the Tote Betting Authorities run only a small percentage of the off-course agencies in their State. The majority of these agencies are operated by franchise on a commission basis. But the Australian bettor, like his American counterpart, is offered many different types of exotic bets like the Trio, naming the three place horses in a race in any order, the Quadrella, naming four winners in selected races and the American-type Trifecta. The New South Wales superbly computerized system is the envy of most of the racing nations in the world with its automatic ticket dispensing totalisators.

All betting in Germany is controlled by the tote whether it be on-course or off-course although bookmakers do exist and are not illegal. The Tote Indicator Boards on the racecourses show the money being wagered off the course as well as the money being played by the racegoers. The various types of bet are similar to those offered in France and the USA and dividends are declared to a DM10 unit.

The *Rennquintett* is West Germany's version of the French *tiercé* but the bettor must name the first five horses in a nominated race of 18 runners and 10% of this pool is ploughed back into racing and breeding.

A section of the crowd in the betting ring at Australia's most important race—the Melbourne Cup.

Index

*The figures in **bold** refer to colour plates. Those in italics refer to the page numbers of black and white illustrations. Other figures refer to text pages.*